Build Your Own

Low-Cost

Timber and Beam

House

William H. Stephens

Authors Book Nook

Thanks to Joe Baker for his computer graphics enhancement
of both the diagrams and photos

Authors Book Nook

Foreword

I love wood. I love its various textures. I love to see the grain emerge as it is finished. I love to touch its smooth surfaces.

For these reasons and more, I prefer the timber and beam over the log house. The log house is more rustic, the interior and exterior walls are the same, the grain in the wood is much less clear unless the logs are squared and planed, and the interior of the house is darker.

A timber and beam structure is more tailored and enables the builder to attach siding of his choice between the beams and to finish the interior to his liking. The house is more tailored inside and out, and the exposed wood stands in contrast to the wall finish between the beams.

If these realities strike your fancy, this book should help you bring your dream to reality. The cost of my 1200-square-foot house, not counting land, was about $22,000.

Chapter 1
Finding Materials,
Designing, and
Getting Started

A Log Cabin for Practice

I drifted into my preference for timber and beam by first building a one-room log cabin. In 1979, my wife Shirley and I purchased twenty-one acres about thirty miles from our home. We live on the south edge of Nashville, Tennessee, and so our land was well out into the countryside. It was generally flat, gently sloping toward the paved county road that borders it on the south. About half of the acreage is covered with hardwoods and cedars.

If you are at the stage of looking for timbered land, make sure the timber rights have not already been sold. Our search led us to several places we liked, but the farmers had sold the marketable wood already. Had we not checked the deed each time, we would have purchased land only to have a lumber company tear up the forest floor with their machinery and leave only small trees standing.

Once you own your property, scout the land well until you know it thoroughly. Walk every bit of it, through the tangles of undergrowth and difficult terrain. Watch for signs of water runoff. You will not want to build in such a place; if you set your heart on a site even slightly lower than the surrounding land, you will need to divert the rivulets that develop during rainfall.

I intended from the first to build a house, but I had never tackled such a project before and decided to learn by building a small cabin. Shirley and I decided we wanted it to be located deep in the woods, far away from any road activity.

We were on a tight budget at the time, and the only tools we could afford were typical hand tools. But never mind, I had the pioneer spirit. We choose a site some 1400 feet from the road and across two stream beds. Some of the property was open, but the last 400 feet or so was through thick woods. Anxious to get started on the cabin, I had to park my car on the road side of the first stream, which is perennial. I dropped a foot log over the gulch and lugged my supplies about a quarter mile each time I worked, fighting my way through trees and brush. I cleared the site with an axe, taking several Saturdays to do so.

I soon realized my efforts were taking up a lot of time. Two things were apparent. First, I would save time in the long run by providing myself better access to the building site; second, I badly needed a chain saw. I purchased an inexpensive "homeowner" type with a sixteen-inch chain. It worked fine for a while, but when it became hot it simply would not run. I had to set it aside to cool down for an hour or two before I could proceed. Of course, there is always a lot to do while you wait, but your work flow is interrupted. After a year or so of this aggravation, I bought a Stihl. It has never stopped on me from overheating. My advice: Get a good chain saw the first time.

To develop access to the cabin site, I had to construct a bridge of some sort over the creek. I needed a culvert, but could not afford one. To solve the problem, I cut a number of small cedars ranging in thickness from 1 1/2 to 2 1/2 inches and cut them into eighteen-inch lengths. I nailed them together into a square culvert, eighteen inches on each side and ten feet long. I set it carefully onto the bottom of the creekbed, filled dirt up to its top and tamped it down good, spanned across the culvert with large flat rocks to divert some of the weight, then finished covering it with dirt and rock. I have had to replace the dirt four or five times due to rainfall, but it is still functioning almost twenty years later. Plastic sheeting over the culvert probably would have eliminated this problem. Someday, I'm going to do the job right. The stream usually is low enough for the culvert to carry the water load, but when a good rain comes, the crossover becomes a spillway.

The culvert enabled me to drive within 400 feet or so of my cabin site except when the land was muddy. The next task was to clear a road through the dense woods. My son Greg, a teenager then, was a big help with this phase. We mapped a slightly curving lane to avoid cutting down the largest trees. I wanted to construct the cabin of cedars, and we gained a few logs during this process. Most of the trees were hickory, oak, elm, and ash, though, so we had a lot of firewood but no fireplace. Some of our friends were delighted. Our makeshift lane worked fine, but when a low area became marshy in wet weather I could not take a vehicle

5

across. Later, I dug a pond with a Bobcat and used the excavation dirt and rock to fill in the marsh.

When we completed the road we were able to start the cabin in earnest. After taking an inventory of available cedars on the land, we decided the maximum length of log would be sixteen feet. Our supply determined the cabin's size.

The first task was to set the vertical logs on which the foundation "sill logs" would rest. We selected the thickest cedars we could find and set them about thirty inches into the ground. Alerted by some book or article, we placed the small end down. If the large end points down, the weight of the cabin rests completely on the butt of the log. Inverted, the weight is distributed all along the sides of the log as well as on the butt. We took the precaution of placing a large flat rock in the bottom of each hole and saturating the fill dirt with chlordane (unavailable now by law). Also, an old farmer's tale claims that termites will not be a problem if the structure is at least eighteen inches above ground. Whether this is true or not, we took the precaution.

The foundation absolutely must be level. Take great pains with this step. It will save you much grief in every succeeding operation. I made a water level from clear plastic hose which I purchased at a building supply store. Just about any diameter will work, but the larger it is the easier it is to get out all the air bubbles. The level is accurate only if cleared of bubbles.

With my foundation piers set to the approximate height above ground I desired, I tied each end of the hose to a corner post and filled the hose with water until the level was at the height I wanted the piers to be. I doublechecked by measuring the corner logs on the same sides each way and the ones diagonally opposite, made my final marks, and cut the tops by the cedars off. I was ready to go up with the cabin.

If your use cedar logs, skin them when the sap is up. They skin quickly and easily then, but are very difficult when the sap is down. Shirley isn't into construction work, but she liked skinning cedars and did a lot of them. My experience with hardwoods was that they are very difficult to bark. You will save time by squaring them off with a chainsaw, eliminating the bark in the process. I have had no experience with pine.

This book is about building a timber and beam house, so I will leave the log cabin at this point. If you want to follow my procedure and build a small structure for both practice and enjoyment, several how-to books are on the market. It took me about a hundred cedar logs and five years to build this cabin, using Saturdays, some afternoons, and occasional holidays.

I considered building a cordwood house for several reasons. They entail little waste of material, the pieces are small and therefore lightweight, and the appearance is pleasing. Several books are on the market to tell about this construction method. To check the feasibility, I built a six-foot square structure in which I placed a commode. Two large plastic garbage cans catch rainwater from the roof, which is piped to the commode tank. The water pressure is not great enough to work the valve, so the tank has to be filled by turning the water supply on and off. The septic system also was made with plastic garbage containers, one to catch the waste, another filled with small rocks to catch the overflow. Our cabin way back in the woods has a flush toilet next to it. Talk about luxury!

The cordwood structure is not to my liking. It makes a good outbuilding, but is difficult if not impossible to make weather tight. Moreover, I found that I do not enjoy working with masonry nearly as much as with wood.

As time went on, we held family gatherings and church socials at the cabin. Many wonderful memories surround the place, and we still use it from time to time. Those preliminary structures, however, guided us toward the timber and beam method.

Choosing the Site

Shirley and I considered a site deep in the woods to be ideal for a log cabin. Originally, we planned for the larger structure to be built next to the cabin and tied to it with a dog run. The remoteness of the site has its advantages, but it has two strong disadvantages. First, utilities would be very difficult and expensive to run that far from the road. Second, we discovered that the air is considerably cooler in more open areas. The dense woods block any breeze at all. During summer days, even in the forest shade, the heat can be oppressive.

We decided on a site among some trees about 450 feet from the county road. It has good shade and privacy, but a slight breeze almost always blows across the semi-open meadow. We were fortunate in having city water come to the area, and electricity is available without paying extra for additional poles (thanks to our good neighbors, the Kendricks, who allowed a pole to be placed on their land).

Finding the Logs

If you have timber on your land, your own stock obviously is the cheapest source for logs. My original intention was to harvest the supply from our land. Our property has very little softwood except cedar, so I decided to use oak and ash. I inventoried the stock by walking the acreage systematically with a clipboard and noting every tree that was large enough to produce beams. I marked them with red plastic tape, which can be purchased at a building supply store. This done, Greg and I began cutting trees. We had considerable experience at this, but oaks are very heavy. We soon realized that harvesting enough for our purpose would take a very long time. I decided to supplement the supply by purchasing one or more log houses.

Old log cabins and houses still can be found, sometimes already dismantled and numbered, but the cost is rising. We watched newspapers and the *Trader's Post,* a classified ad publication, and made several trips to look at advertised materials. These trips usually took at least an afternoon, as most of the supply is well out into the country. Finally, we ran into a bit of luck due to someone else's bad luck.

A lawyer and his wife contracted with a sawmill to cut a supply of poplar logs for a house they intended to build. Their instructions were to cut the logs flat on opposite sides to leave a thickness of eight inches. This procedure, they reasoned, would give them a flat surface inside and out, with filler between the logs covering the rounded ends.

The problem would have been foreseeable by anyone with log

experience. As the logs cured, checking occurred on the cut sides, leaving large cracks in most of the logs. Since these sides were to be exposed, the logs were unfit for his use. I looked over the supply carefully and decided I could cut around the checks and get two beams out of most of the logs. I made a bid of $3900, about half what the sawmill had charged to cut them, including delivery to our land about seventy miles away. My offer was accepted, so I had my supply at one fell swoop.

Poplar is a good wood for either a log or timber and beam house. It is strong and the trees are straight, the grain is pleasing, and it is easy to work. The sapwood is about the color of pine, the heartwood almost as red as cedar.

We had already designed our house. It was not to be a home, but rather an office and a retreat. Up until we purchased the logs, our plan had been a simple one-story structure, a large room with a kitchen and bath. What appeared to be a plentiful supply of timber caused us to revise our design to a high-pitched roof with gables on each end. The upstairs story formed by the roof pitch was to contain two bedrooms and a bath, the downstairs a large open room, a kitchen, and a bath, about 1600 feet altogether. However, after nearly completing the framing for the first story, I realized I had more waste than I had anticipated. The high-pitched roof required 24-foot rafters. I did not have nearly enough logs that would yield sufficient rafters of that length. I was forced to redesign the structure.

After careful inventory, and with the experience I had gained thus far, I shifted the design to the one shown in this book. The floor space was reduced to about 1200 feet, but the basic purpose of the house remained the same. The redesign lost a bedroom but still has one bedroom, two baths, and is considerably larger than our original plans.

Plan your structure carefully before you purchase a log supply or begin shaping your logs into beams. You may have to alter your plans, but you will save much time and material if you know what you want. I found that looking at floor plans was a good aid. Floor plan magazines may be purchased in bookstores and floor plan books may be checked out of a library or purchased. These sources brought features to mind I might not otherwise have thought of. Even so, I still found it preferable to develop a plan designed specifically for our use.

Cutting the Logs

To cut the logs to size, I had two choices. I could haul them to a sawmill, which at the time would have charged 15 cents a running foot. The other choice was to purchase a sawmill and do the work myself. With my pioneer spirit in high gear, I made the second choice. In log-building magazines, I checked the advertisements of one-man sawmills and ordered information on all that appeared feasible for my operation. Cost, ease of handling, and amount of kerf lost were my primary considerations. I chose the RipSaw Mini Mill from Better Built Corporation as the best choice. It has a maximum cut of 9" in height and 14" in width and weighs less than 50 pounds, light enough for one man to handle. The price is within reason, and since it uses a bandsaw blade it takes a very small kerf.

A cheaper type of sawmill is the kind that attaches to a chainsaw blade. I used one of these for the cabin in the woods. It worked all right for that purpose but took a large kerf and was much slower. Better Built's address is 789 Woburn Street, Wilmington, MA 01887.

I learned several things about using this sawmill that I wish I had known sooner. Here are some pointers you otherwise would have to learn the hard way.

1. If you have electricity available, I recommend that you purchase the sawmill with an electric motor. It is quieter, less jolting to use, requires less maintenance, and does not require constant refilling with oil and gas. The gas engine is a Stihl chain saw engine modified with gears to fit the sawmill. This is what I purchased because I did not have electricity when I began the project.

2. If you have a shed, store your stock out of the weather. Place a row of small logs or lumber to raise the stock off the ground enough for air to pass under, and place two- or three-inch thick separators between each layer. Or criss-cross alternate layers of logs. As best you can figure, stack the logs in the order you will need them.

3. I had a serious, unanticipated problem with my finished beams. They bowed. To make straight beams, I wasted some good wood. I finally learned that if I cut the log down the cracks, the bowing was minimized. Apparently, the wood tends to bow away from the cracks but the remaining fibers prevent this. When I cut the logs into beams, the wood did what it was trying to do. After this initial cut, I allowed two or three days for each cut to bow however it wanted to, then cut my beams to proper thickness. This process requires an extra cut on the sawmill but will save you a great deal of planing later.

4. Cut your supply as you need it for each step. I began by intending to cut and stack the entire supply. The job became exceedingly

boring. Moreover, if you change your mind about some design matter that requires different dimensions of beams, you have locked yourself in.

5. Do not continue to use the blade after it becomes dull in an attempt to get a little more mileage out of it. Apart from the extra muscle a dull blade requires, it begins to waffle. A dull blade will try to go around knotholes and tight grain, leaving you with a wavy finish you will have to level with a planer. The manufacturer sells blades that can be sharpened, but I found that purchasing new ones from a sawblade manufacturer is easier and probably about as cheap. These blades cannot be sharpened. They are bandsaw blades, made to your specifications. I ordered 90-inch bands, 3/4 inch wide, with three teeth to the inch for about $8.00 each. My supplier, handily, was near Nashville. However, they since have gone out of business.

6. Raise the log you intend to cut to a position that will enable you to work without bending. Purchase or arrange for lifting equipment. A hand winch works fine, so long as you have something overhead from which to hang it, such as a beam inside a shed or an A-frame outside. None of my logs were too large for two men to manhandle, though we had to use levers and such. When Greg was available we had no trouble at all. When I worked alone, I needed additional equipment. A tripod, lightweight enough for one man to put into position, is a great help. Raise the log to a workable height without having to bend; stack small log ends or blocks underneath for support. Since the log has rounded edges, you will stabilize it with wedges or blocks of wood.

7. Use safety equipment. Every handyman knows this, but sometimes we take chances. A chip in the eye is not worth the time saved. Wear a dust mask and goggles. If you can't wear that combination

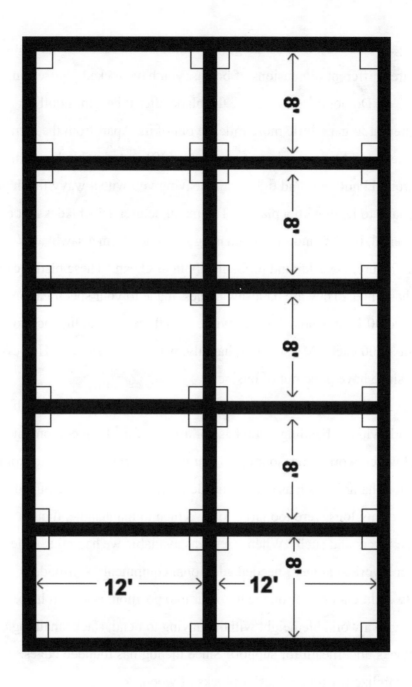

Diagram 1

14

because your goggles fog up, wear a kerchief over your nose and mouth. Also, keep a back brace handy and put it on each time you lift a heavy weight. These can be purchased at many building supply stores for $15-$20. (Don't expect to be superman just because you wear a back brace; don't lift more than is reasonable for you.)

Laying the Foundation

I made the mistake of choosing a pier and beam foundation. If I had it to do over again, I would lay a continuous foundation. A continuous foundation usually is made of cinder block and runs continuously around the perimeter of the planned structure. Many books are available to tell you how to build this type. In this section, I will describe the method I followed.

The pier and beam is fine structurally. My choice was based on cost and my mistaken idea that it would be easier to construct this type than the continuous. I rented a small backhoe to dig the holes and wound up digging continuous trenches anyway. Moreover, I realized later that a continuous foundation would be more attractive and would provide better insulation. In fact, I wound up filling in between the piers, as you will see later.

I built my forms out of plywood, fourteen inches square and thirty inches deep or on bedrock. I set the piers for the long sides of the building eight feet apart on center; the piers for the short sides are twelve feet apart, a single center one between the corner piers. Another row of piers runs down the center lengthwise, eight feet apart and in line with the outside piers (diagram 1). The interior piers are ten inches square, since they carry only floor weight and not walls. With the forms carefully set, Greg and I refilled the open trenches around them with dirt and rock to hold them securely in place. The next step was to level the forms. Using a water level as described above, we marked each form, then drew a level line around the form. We cut off the excess wood with a reciprocating saw.

Rather than build forms from plywood, you may opt to purchase thick cardboard tubes from a supplier. The tubes are put in place and cut to level just like the plywood forms. They save time, but your forms are round rather than square, which might be a visual problem to you.

We filled the forms to their tops with concrete. By this time, I had electricity to the site and rented a mixer with an electric motor. To purchase concrete by the sack runs up the cost considerably, so Greg and I hauled sand by pickup truck from a lumberyard and purchased sacks of portland cement. Rather than gravel, we used rocks gathered from our property. Our mixture was one part cement to three parts sand, plus rocks which we added as we filled the forms. If you use rocks rather than gravel, lean toward a richer rather than a leaner mix (more rather than less cement). As you add the water, remember that the mixture should be fairly thick so the rocks will not sink to the bottom.

I do not like to work in cold weather. We had all kinds of unforeseen difficulties due to rain and low temperatures after we began setting our foundation. Though there are ways to pour concrete in temperatures below freezing, we did not want to do so. It was well into December when we finished the job, and that fall we had more rain than usual.

Layers of limestone underlay the ground throughout our region. We had to break through some of this stone in order to sink our foundations below the freeze line, 18 inches in our area. During rains, water collects on the limestone layers and finds the low places, which happened to be the excavation trenches for our foundation. Greg and I spent considerable effort bailing and pumping water from our forms. Do not try to pour your concrete mix through the water. The sand will separate and your mix will be ruined. We had to work fast once the water was removed, since it kept seeping back in. We only finished the job well after dark when the temperature had fallen into the thirties. Both of us were pretty sure we would catch terrible colds from the ordeal. We were right.

As we filled each form, we worked long bolts head-down into the mix, with ten inches protruding above the concrete (photo 2). You will need to purchase 12 to 14 inch bolts. The bolts secure both the horizontal and the vertical beams to the piers. Later, you will drill holes into the beams to accommodate the bolts. Since you want your beams to run along the outside edge of the piers, set the bolts to position the beams accordingly. Do not leave a ledge of concrete on which water can accumulate. With  the sill beams at the outside edge of the piers, several inches of surface will remain on the inward side. Crossbeams will rest on these surfaces.

With the piers set, we let our bodies rest for the winter. The next spring we began building the frame.

Getting Utilities
At the earliest possible time, you should set up a temporary electrical construction post. This temporary electrical service is controlled by code and must be

built to specifications. You will need to place it in line with the final wires coming from your electrical utility company, so your plans for where the electrical supply will enter your house should be firm. Call the utility company that serves the area where you are building and have a representative come out to advise you. Also, it probably has a drawing with instructions.

The Duck River Utility Cooperative that serves Marshall County, Tennessee--where our new use is located—provides two permanent telephone poles. More are extra. The closest available electricity was on my neighbor's property. The Kindricks' kindly agreed to allow the connection, even though it required another pole near their drive. That pole and one more on my property was sufficient.

The temporary construction pole requires a weatherhead, conduit and connections, a breaker box, and outdoor electrical outlets. We connected two exterior duplexes with GFCI plugs to the breaker box, giving us four outlets for plugs.

After discussing the location with your utility representative, install the temporary service and call your electrical inspector to have it approved. He works for the state but is in close touch with the utility company so you can call them to find out how to make an appointment. Once the inspector has approved your temporary service, the utility will turn on the electricity.

After you have the building under roof, you probably will want to make extension cords from # 12 wiring approved for outdoor use. Use 2-wire plus ground. Greg and I used extension cords until we raised the walls; then we ran two wires from the duplexes on the service pole up to the top of the pole and then to the house, bringing them in just under the roofline. The wires were out of the way and we attached them securely. We then wrapped the boxes on the pole in plastic to protect them from weather. From then on we could work under roof even during heavy rains without danger.

Chapter 2

Constructing the Sills

A timber and beam home is basically a framework built of squared timbers, the framework then being filled in with whatever material one may choose. One ancient English version uses dirt as fill. Those industrious folk built forms between the beams and tamped dirt down into the forms, removed the forms, and covered the hard-packed dirt surface with a thick coat of plaster. This style usually has diagonal beams added to support the fill.

In modern timber and beam styles, the spaces between the vertical beams are filled with traditional sidings and insulation (photo 1/cover). Of course, it all starts at the bottom.

The outside sills

Sill beams are the first run of beams, which in effect becomes the foundation on which the structure rests. Greg and I set the long sides first. You can use a variety of beam lengths for the sills, so long as each length spans from one pier to the next. The longer the beams, of course, the less fitting you have to do. For us, each long side consisted of three beams, two of them 16 feet, 3 inches long and one 8 feet 3 inches long, to produce a total length of forty feet.

corner   corner

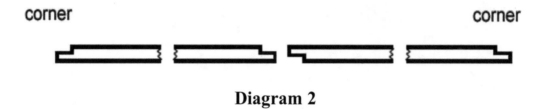

Diagram 2

The extra three inches on each beam is for overlap (diagram 2).

I figured a six-inch overlap on all connecting beams running the same direction. For connecting beams at the corners, I figured the overlap equal to the width of the beam. I cut my sill beams to be 6 x 8's, so the corner overlap also was six inches, adjusted to 5 1/2 inches after planing (photo 2).

When you are ready to cut your beams, double check the measurements from one bolt anchored in concrete to the next. Ideally, your beams should run three inches beyond each embedded bolt. If your bolts are off a bit, you have only to determine where to drill your holes. Three inches is somewhat arbitrary, but the bolt should not be too near the end of a beam.

To fit the sill beams for the shorter sides of the structure, measure the same way, except note that the beams span twelve feet from the edge of the outside pier to the center of the middle pier. As before, add three inches to each of the end beams to allow for a six-inch overlap. This wider spacing on the ends was because my original plan called for the roof weight to rest on the long walls; the end sills were intended to carry only the weight of the end walls. When I had to change my plans due to inventory, my piers were already laid. To avoid having too much roof weight on the end sills, I used "king poles," which I will explain at the proper time.

Once you have cut your beams to the right length, the next step obviously is to finish and notch them. If you want a rough finish, with sawtooth marks, you are ready to notch as soon as you cut the beam. If you want a smoother appearance, you will need to plane your beams. The sawmill I used leaves a much smoother cut than does a chainsaw mill, but not as smooth as I wanted. This is a matter of taste.

If your beams warp any at all (and they probably will), your best course will be to plane them, which you may have to do at any rate to make them completely straight. A finish edger-planer that has say a 4-foot table will take a bow out of a beam, but it is limited to a width of six inches. The other type of tabletop planer has only a 12-inch or so resting surface, with the blades adjustable by crank to cut the top surface rather than the bottom. It will give you a uniform thickness which the edger-planer will not do, but it will not remove a bow. All things considered, it is the best choice if you purchase only one planer. To remove a bow, use a long straightedge to mark along each edge of the beam, then shave off any excess wood with a hand (power) planer. You need to eliminate high spots; you also need to keep each surface square to the adjoining one.

If your beams are not bowed, a table planer is the most efficient way to smooth them, provided you have some help. Remember that this tool will make opposite sides exactly parallel to each other but will not square adjoining sides. Check for square and straighten with a hand planer. The table planer I purchased has a capacity of nine inches in height and fourteen inches in width. My sill beams were six by eight, reduced to 5 1/2 by 7 1/2 when finished.

I intended to run these beams through the planer, but even using "dead man" rollers on each end, I found the beams too difficult to handle. You definitely need another live body for this task. Working alone, I wound up using an electric hand planer. The job is not perfect; little ridges remain in the wood due to the width of the planer blade, but they are hardly noticeable with the sealer and stain applied.

With your beams squared and planed, the overlaps next have to be prepared. Cut the ends of each beam half the depth of the beam's thick side. Since my beams ended up being 5 1/2 inches x 7 1/2 inches, I removed a section of wood 3 3/4 inches deep for the vertical cut. The horizontal cut was 5 ½ inches. Use a tri-square to mark your lines, then use a circular saw to cut as deep as the blade will go, following the lines on three sides. This cut provides a guide for a less accurate saw. If you have a small chainsaw and are pretty good with it, you might finish the cut with it. I prefer an electric rather than a gas chainsaw for this type work. Otherwise, the slower reciprocating saw may be used, or a good hand saw is more accurate. To obtain an exact fit, make the cut a bit shy of the mark and finish it to exact proportions with a wide chisel or slick. (A slick is a long-handled chisel, with a blade about three inches wide.) Unless you can find a slick in a flea market, which I never did, you will have to order it through a specialty house for about $35-$50. Rather than make that investment, I used a 2 1/2-inch chisel and a wood mallet, which I did find in a flea market.

Be sure to plan each notch to fit its neighbor (diagram 2). Your first long side beam should be notched for an underlap on both ends. The first notch for the next beam will overlap the previous beam and underlap the next one. The end at the corner needs to be an underlap. In other words, whichever beam is set in place first should be an underlap to allow the next beam to overlap it. Set the beams on top of the concrete piers to provide a level work area as you trim the notches.

Before you set the beams, you should stain them with a protective coating. Unless you want to use creosote, I know of no satisfactory treatment that will make your wood completely safe from bugs. Since bugs eat cellulose, sealing off the supply is a reasonable alternative. I used Behr's Natural Seal Plus No. 82, which I thought at the time was the best I could find. It turned out to mildew badly on exposed surfaces after about two years. I applied three coats on all four sides. The first coat is absorbed quickly, and each coat needs to go on while the former coat is still a bit damp. The butt ends absorb a lot of liquid and should be painted again and again. In addition, I poured preservative into cracks in the wood and let it soak in. I applied the treatment to every beam in the house that would be exposed to the weather, before I set it into place. I left the inside surfaces bare so as to use finishes appropriate to inside exposures.

Once you are satisfied with your notches and the stain has dried, you are ready to set the beams onto the piers. To do so, you will have to locate where to drill the holes. If two men are available, set the beams on top of the bolts and position them exactly by using a level, touching it to the outside of the concrete piers and the outside of the beam. One man can hold the beam into place, balanced on top of the bolts, while the other draws a circle around the bolt from below. This method is the most accurate, but if you are working alone, an alternative method is to set the beam in place onto the surface of the piers and shoved against the bolts. Measure from the outside of the pier to the bolt and then measure in from the side of the beam the same distance. The placement of these bolt holes is critical. If your measurement is off only slightly, you will have a bend in your wall line. So if your hole is not drilled right on the money, you should make the hole larger in whichever direction is necessary for correction.

The outside beams on the short sides of the house are 12 feet, 3 inches in length; with a 6-inch overlap at the center, the total length of an end being 24 feet. For the center overlap, it does not matter which end is on top and which is on bottom. For the ends, be sure the overlap is on top so it will lay onto the end beam, assuming you lay the long sides first.

The center sills

The center run of beams tie into the sill beams at the center of each end. A mortise and tenon joint is used for this connection. I did not make this cut into the end beams until I was ready to set the center run. Eight-foot-plus beams work fine for the center run. Figure a six-inch overlap except at each end where the run is mortised two inches into the sills.

Beauty and strength are two reasons why the center connection should not go all the way through the beam. You don't want a bunch of butt ends showing all along the sill beams when the house is finished, and the weakening effect of cutting away half the depth of the sill beams is obvious.

The mortise and tenon cut may be done in several ways. The simplest is to cut a notch on the end of the beam that joins the end sill, leaving two inches thickness at the top and the full width of the beam. The mortise cut into the end still will match. Secure the joint with a barn nail or large screw, for which you first should drill a hole.

You may also choose a narrower and deeper mortise and tenon. The tenon may be as narrow as two inches by three inches deep, again secured with a screw or barn nail. Diagram 3 pictures the strongest joint, with a modified V shape and an upslant on the bottom. It takes longer to cut but does not require a nail or screw; once the floor is down, the joint cannot turn loose. All the beam ends, by the way, rest on concrete piers, so no strength is lost.

Floor beams

With the sill beams set around the perimeter of the foundation piers and

26

the center run of beams in place, you are ready to set the floor beams. These beams will support your floor joists. You have a choice of setting your floor joists on top of these beams or attaching them to the sides of the beams, making the joist tops even with the tops of the beams. Laying the floor joists will come much later in the process, but you need to decide now which process to follow. Your choice will determine the length of your vertical beams, which will set upright on the sill beams. Assuming you plan for eight-foot ceilings, you must add the height of the joist if you plan to set them on top of the floor beams.

You do not need to be particular about dressing the sides of the floor beams if you plan to set your floor joists on top of them. If you plan to make your joists level with the floor beams, you have two choices of how to attach them. You can mortise and tenon the joints into the beams. This allows you to leave the logs rounded on the sides and bottom, since you can cut your mortises into the rounds, though it will be easier is you flatten them roughly where they attach. This can be done quickly with a chain saw. If you choose to butt the joists against the beam sides and attach them with nails, screws, or other hardware, you will save time by dressing the beam sides evenly. My choice was to set the floor joists on top of the beams. This process took less work and gave me more height for the crawl space. Consequently, to end up with 8-foot walls, you might make your vertical beams (later) 8' 7 1/2", figuring 2 x 8s for the joists. Or, if your ceiling is to be set above the upper beam (7 1/2" thick), the verticals can be 8'.

You should set your floor beams not more than eight feet apart (diagram 1). They will run from the side sill beams to the center beams. The span, obviously, is almost twelve feet. Here is the way I determined placement of the beams, measuring down the long side of the structure: To allow room to attach siding, I placed the end of my tape one inch from the outside corner and marked

27

off eight-foot increments on center. The one-inch inset resulted in each of my crossbeams being a bit off center from the bolts embedded in the piers. This worked out fine, because the offset allowed me more leeway to avoid the bolts when I cut the mortises for the crossbeams, as I will explain. If you follow this procedure, take measurements from both ends of the house on each side and also down the center beams. Since your measurements begin one inch from each corner, the marks coming from opposite ends will not coincide; they will be an inch or two apart. Halfway between them is the centerpoint for your beam. Lay a straightedge of some sort from a mark on the sill beam to the corresponding mark on the center beam and stand off to observe. If your sill beams are set exactly right, the straightedge will be at a right angle to the sill. If you are off a bit, you will know it at this point. In that case, you probably are close enough to adjust your floor beams without serious problems by sliding one end over just a bit. Be sure you set the floor beams at 90 degrees to the sills.

The ends of the floor beams must rest on the concrete piers, which are wide enough that this will not be a problem. Cut each floor beam to allow for two inches of overlap on both the sill beam and the center beam.

To tie the framing together securely, I used a wedge type mortise and tenon (diagram 3). I also cut a downward wedge. This style provides enough side pressure so that the floor beams will not work up, especially after the floor

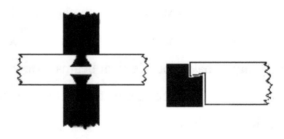

Diagram 3

is laid, and certainly will not pull out. For an easier cut, eliminate the wedge. A straight cut will be satisfactory if you secure it with a long screw or a barn nail. Cut your floor beam tenons first, before you cut the mortise; you will mark the mortise cut by tracing around the tenon.

Since the floor beams will rest on the concrete piers, they must be the same thickness as the sill beams, and the mortise and tenons must match exactly. With the topside of the beam up, measure back two inches and make a light mark across the beam. Using a tri-square, measure down each side three inches from the mark. Remember that you are going to cut away the bottom, leaving the top as a tenon, so avoid marking where you do not want to cut. Start your downward mark three inches below the top and continue it to the bottom of the log. Do the same on the opposite side. Turn the beam over and connect the lines on each side. Mark across the butt end of the beam three inches down. Then draw a line on each side to connect the marks on the sides and butt. I found it helpful to mark with XXX the portion to be cut away; it is very easy to make a mistake. Cut away the bottom portion. The tenon will measure 2 inches back from the butt and 3 inches deep.

The plan I used for the tenon was to add a downward slope of 1/2 inch to add grip strength. If you follow this plan, mark the back of the projection 1/2 inch up from the bottom of your former cut, then on each side of the tenon draw a connecting line from the point of the projection to the 1/2 inch mark. Cut this small wedge away first with a circular saw, then finish it with a reciprocating or hand saw.

If you use the squared tenon, you will secure it into the mortise with a screw or barn nail. If you use the wedge, you will need no other fastener.

Set the prepared floor beam on top of the sill beams and mark the tenon onto the sill beams. Use a tri-square to continue this mark down the side to a depth of 2 1/2 inches for the wedge or 3 inches for the squared tenon. Your finished mark should have you cutting two inches into the top of the sill beam and down its side for 2 1/2 inches.

Use a chain saw to roughcut the mortise, following the shape of the tenon. With a sharp chisel, clean out the exact dimensions. Next, if you use the downward wedge, you will cut a 1/2 inch slope into the bottom of the cutout. This cut is difficult but will become easier with practice. If you are careful, you can use a reciprocating saw to cut the sides of the wedge, which is cross grain. Be careful not to go too fast or you will jam your sawblade. Chisel out the wedge, using chisels of various widths, for the mortise.

Chapter 3

Constructing the First-Story Walls

With the sill beams and cross beams completed, you can begin to visualize the shape of the house. The next step was to construct the wall framing.

Center frame

We began with the center frame, the section that runs down the center of the house lengthwise. It is 32 feet in length, not counting the porch, and is a simple construction. We built half of it, a 16-foot section, using the sills for a level work surface. Then we raised it by use of a winch.

The section consists of only three pieces, but they are very heavy: a 16-foot span supported at each end by an 8 x 8 vertical (diagram 4). Our design called for a large open room; we did not want a center column to interfere.

The ends of the vertical beams are square, no cutouts on either the tops or bottoms. The horizontal, though, will connect in the center with another 16-foot beam and so the ends must be prepared. Other crossbeams will be attached later.

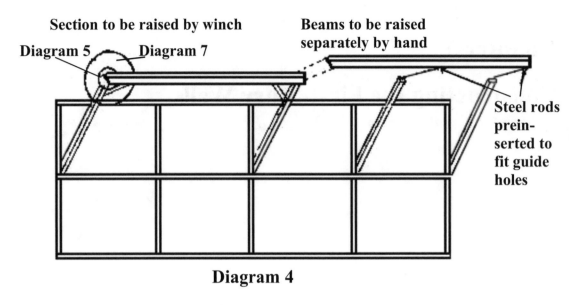

Section to be raised by winch

Beams to be raised separately by hand

Diagram 5   Diagram 7

Steel rods prein-serted to fit guide holes

Diagram 4

Some of the cuts are better done now. Others for the second-story floor joists or connecting beams (depending on your design) can be done either at this stage or later. If you are absolutely sure you won't change your design as you progress, make all cuts at this stage before the beam is raised. These and other cuts are described in later chapters. For now, we will focus only on the ends of the beams.

Previous overlaps, for the sill beams, were 6 inches; these will be 3 3/4 inches. The reason for the shorter cut is to allow at least two inches of the full thickness of these beams, plus the overlapping portions, to rest onto the vertical. In diagram 5, you can see how the beam ends are notched at this stage. The left end will have another beam for the porch structure to be tied in at a later stage. To allow for two inches of vertical surface on which the porch beam will rest, the 16' beam must be inset 2" onto the left vertical. The finished length of this long span consequently is 15' 11 3/4". The notch is cut shallow enough that the full thickness of the horizontal will rest on the vertical beam for two inches in addition to the overlap.

Beams will connect at right angles to both horizontals. They too must rest on the verticals for strength. To accommodate the cross connections, the overlaps will butt against one another from each direction (diagram 5). The overlap you leave on each end of the horizontal will measure 3 3/4"s x 3 3/4".

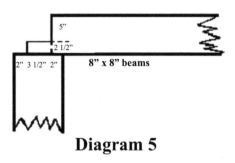

5"

2 1/2"

2" 3 1/2" 2"   8" x 8" beams

Diagram 5

To construct this center section, use the sill beams for a level surface to work on. I constructed the left side first (diagram 4). Position the feet of the verticals exactly where they will be located when raised. Set the three pieces into place (the two verticals and the horizontal).

The bolt ends that hold the sill beam to the concrete piers protrude above the sill beams (diagram 6, photo 2). Drill holes into the feet of the two verticals to fit over the bolts. This will secure the vertical beams. Measure carefully and drill so that the bottom of each beam will be exactly where you want them when they are fitted over the bolt ends. Drill a hole the thickness of the bolt and

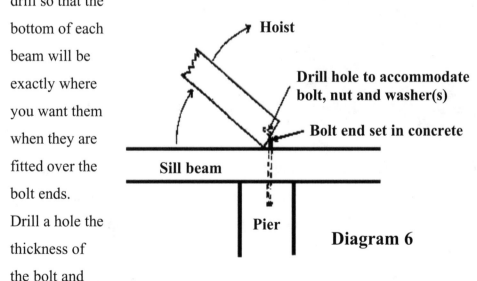

Hoist

Drill hole to accommodate bolt, nut and washer(s)

Bolt end set in concrete

Sill beam

Pier

Diagram 6

just a bit deeper than the bolt protrudes. Then drill out a shallower portion of the hole to accommodate the nut and washer. After drilling the hole, lift the vertical beam into place to be sure it fits snugly down onto the sill beam. Do this for both verticals.

The vertical beams are two inches thicker than the horizontal ones (7 1/2 and 5 1/2"). To accommodate this difference on your work surface, block up the horizontal beam one inch to bring its center to where it will attach to the vertical. One-half-inch iron rods will be used to secure the horizontal to the verticals. Cut them to 6" in length, one for each joint. Position the beams exactly and drill matching holes. Insert the rods and press the beams together until the joint is flush.

The rods maintain the alignment of the beams, but further bracing is essential. Angle braces provide great strength; I set one in each corner (photo 3, diagram 7).

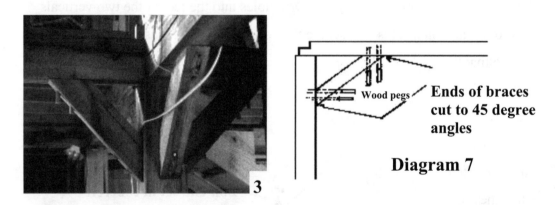

Wood pegs

Ends of braces cut to 45 degree angles

Diagram 7

As shown in the photo, these braces are decorative as well as functional. They secure the wall from lateral movement and are crucial to a well-constructed house. Length can vary; I decided on 24 inches outside measurement, 3 1/2" thick each way.

Cut each end on a 45 degree angle and drill holes for 3/4-inch wooden dowels. The two lower holes should be parallel to the floor, the two upper ones perpendicular when the brace is installed (diagram 7). To be sure you drill

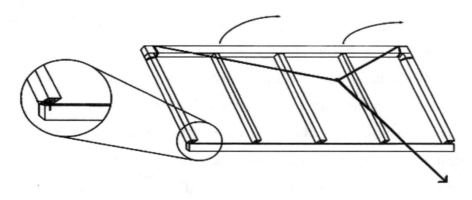

Diagram 8

properly, hold the brace into its corner and make a light mark to indicate the intended direction of the hole. If you want to eliminate spliting or burring of the hole, begin with a 3/4 inch Forster bit on the exposed surface. These bits do not work well for deep holes, though, so once the hole is started you will want to shift to a regular wood bit to finish the job.

Square the horizontal and vertical beams, hold the angle into place, and drill the holes through the brace and on into the beams by running the bit through each hole in the braces. This will produce a consistent angle. The dowel holes must run on a straight line through the brace and into the beam. If slightly off, the brace will twist. Drill three inches deep into each beam. Working alone, I discovered that holding the drill securely enough to drill a straight hole was difficult if I had to hold the brace with one hand. My solution was to attach the brace temporarily with small screws, two on each end. Later, I removed the screws and filled the holes (or you can countersink the holes and leave the screws in).

Cut your pegs a little longer than the sum of the combined hole depth, to allow for splintering when you hammer the rods into place. Apply carpenter's glue to the butt ends of the brace and to each peg, set the brace into its corner, and drive in the peg until it bottoms. Trim off the excess peg material flush with the brace (or leave the trimming job for later).

The frame is ready at this point to be raised into place. Set the feet of each vertical securely against the bolt it will fit over. The bolts serve as pivot points as you raise the structure (diagram 8). The greatest danger in raising the structure is that you might pull it too far, causing it to fall to the other side. Estimate the proper length and tie a guy rope at the top of each end of the structure. Be conservative; if the guys are too short, you can easily lengthen them as the structure nears its raised position. Tie the other end of each guy rope to a sill beam. If you have enough help, each guy rope can be looped around the sill beam and let out by a helper as the structure rises. Be sure your helpers are far enough away to be out of danger in case the winch rope should fail. Advise your helpers their health is worth more than the structure. Always choose personal safety over damage to materials.

One winch is sufficient to hoist the frame, provided the ropes are attached properly. Locate the weight center on the horizontal beam. If your beams are cut uniformly, the weight center will be at the exact center. If your beam is undressed on one or more sides, set a fulcrum under the horizontal at the approximate weight center and move it back and forth until the structure is balanced. Before you hoist the structure, reinforce it with ropes. Run a rope the length of the horizontal beam just below it to secure the verticals tightly. I suggest you use jute or polyester rope rather than nylon. Nylon is very strong, but it stretches. Polyester stretches, too, but not as much. Jute is best if the rope is not weakened with age.

Set a pulley higher than the frame will be when it is raised, if possible. The system will work if the pulley is a bit lower, but the lower you set it the more your line of pull will be against the bolts. In such a case, you may have to partially lift the structure by hand to get it started. Attach the winch rope onto the rope that stretches from vertical to vertical, at the weight center point. Do not attach the winch rope to the structure itself.

When the frame is raised halfway or so, use a hammer and block of wood to knock the feet of the verticals into place to line up the protruding bolts with their holes. Once the bolt starts into the holes, the frame will not slip. Continue raising the frame until it is in place. Have some lumber ready to support the frame temporarily. They should be at least 1 x 4s and long enough to reach about 2/3 up the verticals and five or six feet back from the feet. The bottom of each temporary brace is nailed into a sill beam. Nail one end of the brace to the vertical, then level the beam before nailing the other end into the sill beam. Two braces will be required for each vertical, one running north and south, one east and west.

The other half of the center frame comes next. We had to raise each beam of this section by hand. Theoretically, a winch will work, though it requires some maneuvering. This was a moot point; we do not have an overhead tree to which we could attach a winch. (You can always rent a winch truck, but I assume you are hoping to save money wherever you can.) The 16-foot horizontal beam was very heavy, but Greg and I figured out a way to handle it ourselves.

This second half also consists of three beams, but differently arranged (diagram 4). There is a horizontal beam to match the previous one. It rests on an 8 x 8 vertical beam at the right end, the already-raised 8 x 8 vertical at the left, and also a 6 x 6 one at the center.

To plan the cut for the right end of this horizontal, look at diagrams 9A and B, to decide if you want a full overlap that will show the butt end or a partial overlap in which the butt end does not go all the way through the upper end beams. The butt-to-show cut is easier. For this cut, two-thirds of the thickness of the beam will be taken off the top, to leave one-third on the bottom the width of the beam. Later, the upper wall beams will be cut accordingly to fit over this tenon. If you do not want the butt to show, cut about two inches off the end and plan to make mortise type cuts in the connecting wall beams later. Note that the upper horizontal beams are set flush with the vertical; no ledge is left since no porch is planned for this end. Be sure to cut the notch to leave the tenon on the bottom side.

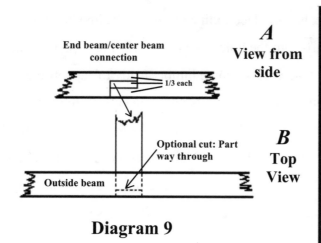

Diagram 9

For the left end of the horizontal, cut the overlap to fit the beam already in place. Notice that one inch remains on each side of the vertical beam on which the transverse beams will rest. As we will discuss later, they do not to carry as much weight and are reinforced with large screws and angle braces.

To prepare to set the outside vertical, cut a hole in its foot to receive the protruding bolt just as you did before, making sure the outside edge of the vertical will be flush with the outside of the sill beam.

The vertical to be attached at the eight-foot point is prepared next. Assuming your sill beams all are 5 1/2 inches wide, locate the point on the center sill beam where the vertical will rest and drill a 1/2-inch hole dead center on the sill beam. Make an X on the bottom of the vertical by drawing lines from opposite corners. Drill the corresponding hole at the crosspoint. Insert the six-inch iron rod into the vertical beam rather than into the sill beam; it is easier to see the hole in the sill beam when you fit the vertical into place.

This wall section is prepared just as was the previous one. Lay the verticals onto a level surface spaced exactly as they will be when raised. Note that you will have to block up both the horizontal and the inside vertical beams one inch to adjust for the thicker vertical on the end. Mark the rod holes at the top ends of the two verticals and the corresponding holes on the horizontal. Drill the holes and drive the rods--in this case--into the tops of the verticals for better visual alignment later.

Set each vertical into place, the outside one over the bolt protruding from the sill beam, the center one into the hole drilled to receive its rod. Level each one and secure them with temporary braces as described above.

Now comes the heavy part. I strongly advise you to wear a back brace as you do this work. You will need to work on a ladder or scaffold in order to guide the horizontal beam into place. Attach the end to the previously raised structure first. Place a ladder against the raised section and tie it securely to prevent it from slipping as you work. For the wall end, make sure the vertical bracing is strong and secure, then tie another ladder to it.

Raise one end of the beam at a time. Do not try to raise the entire beam; it is very heavy and an accident is likely. Lift the inside end onto the overlap prepared for it and tie it tightly into place with rope. For extra help, you might want to fashion a pulley as shown in photo 4, which I did not think of until later. Next, lift the wall end. Though still heavy, much of the weight of the horizontal

39

will be carried on the vertical to which it is tied, so one or two men can handle it.

Have a helper hold the wall end onto its approximate place while you tap the beam with a wooden mallet to line the rods up with their holes.

When both rods are in place, tie the outside end tightly into place and move to the inside end. Work the overlap into exact position, preferably without removing the rope; it is good security against an accident. To receive the attaching screw, drill a guide hole of the proper size through the overlap and a smaller hole through the underlap. Use at least a 6-inch screw--I used a 10-inch--with a bolt head and washer. A ratchet wrench speeds up this task considerably, but be careful not to shear the bolt. You might want to dip the bolt in oil or soap to help overcome the friction (shake off the excess oil).

Recheck the plumb of the verticals and rearrange the temporary braces if necessary. Add angle braces at each end of the horizontal beam (seen through

the window in photo 5), following the procedure previously described. They are not needed at the 6 x 6 beam.

Stand back and admire your work. For the first time, you will have a sense of how impressive your house will be.

First wall frame

Thus far, the placement of windows, doors, and other features has not been discussed. Before you construct the wall frames, you need to decide where every window and door will be and their dimensions. My design called for a 32-inch back door, a 36-inch front door, and a six-foot sliding door opening onto the porch.

I found it helpful to draw an elevation of each wall (diagrams 10-13). You don't have to be an artist to do this; all that is required is straight lines drawn to scale with a ruler. By this time, you surely have considered floor plans and have settled on what you want, including locations of doors and windows. By drawing out each wall, you will discover what adjustments you need to make to accomodate the beams that constitute the frame of your timber and beam house. I set my beams on four-foot centers, beginning the measurements from each corner of the house. The one exception to this was the frame for the sliding door.

The measurements of the vertical beams for the wall are these: Each corner beam is 8 x 8 (7 1/2 x 7 1/2), the same as the three vertical center beams. The sill beams are 5 ½" wide, so with the outsides flush, the inside corner will overlap 2"; this will not show. The beams over the other concrete piers are 6 x 6 (5 1/2 by 5 1/2); they match the width of the sill beams. The finished beams between the piers are 3 1/2 inches wide and 5 1/2 inches deep, the depth again matching the width of the sill beams.

Draw each wall on a separate sheet of paper. Be precise as to scale. Draw the vertical and horizontal beams to dimension, not 8 x 8s, for example, but

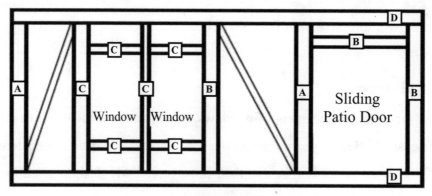

NORTH WALL

Diagram 10

Beam dimensions (All Walls)
A = 8" x 8" (7 1/2" x 7 1/2")   B = 6" x 6" (5 1/2" x 5 1/2")
C = 4" x 6" (3 1/2" x 5 1/2")   D = 6" x 8" (5 1/2" x 7 1/2")

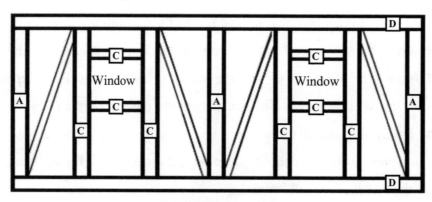

SOUTH WALL

Diagram 11

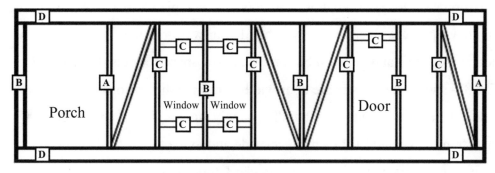

West Wall

Diagram 12

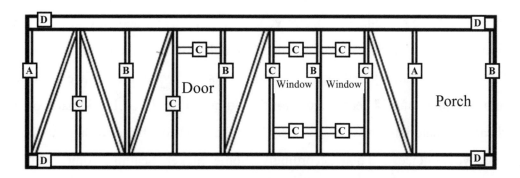

East Wall

Diagram 13

7 1/2 x 7 1/2s. (My upper beams are the same dimensions as my sill beams. Include the angle braces in your drawing (photo 5), which I will explain shortly.

Before you finalize your plans, go to your primary supplier and get measurements for your windows and doors. If you plan to search out used windows, purchase them before you build your wall framing. You are safe with doors; they are standard. Just be sure you allow space for outside measurements. The 32- and 36-inch doors are door widths; framing dimensions must be added. Take a tape measure into your building supply store and measure the doors with their frames, then add 1/2 inch to each side and to the top. I made my own frames and doors, but built them to standard dimensions.

I used a table planer to finish the vertical beams, except for the 8 x 8s, which I finished with the electric hand held planer. If Greg had been available, I would have used the table planer for these, too.

Except for the verticals at each corner of the house, I cut recesses into all four sides of each vertical to receive wallboard on the interior and siding on the exterior (look closely at photo 5). I used a table saw for these cuts, made after the beams were planed. The size of your cuts may vary; it depends on what type siding you use. Plan these recesses deep enough to receive the siding plus the thickness of sheathing material. I made my cuts 3/4" wide (the surface on which to nail siding), and 1" deep (recess for the siding). I used 1/2" blackboard; other sheathing materials run as much as 3/4". Make a trip to a building supply store, make your choice, and plan accordingly. Some thicker sheathing comes with an aluminum covering, which provides better insulation. If you want your siding to protrude beyond the face of the verticals as mine does, or if you prefer the siding to be inset so the verticals protrude, adjust your depth accordingly. I cut the inside and outside of my beams to the same dimensions. The depth inside allowed the sheetrock to be inset and the beams to protrude slightly. Your interior finish work will be much simpler if the vertical surfaces protrude.

Notice the corner-to-corner diagonal braces between the verticals (photo 5). These braces are needed for lateral stability, but they also transfer the weight of the roof onto the piers. They are most important at the corners, so you should not plan a door or window in those four-foot sections. The exception I made is at the sliding door, but that wall carries no roof weight.

If at all possible, plan to build each wall frame flat and raise it as a unit, either whole or in halves just as with the center structure. How you do this depends on how much help you have and whether you have large trees to which you can attach pulleys. For the long walls, you can use the center frame for your pulley(s) if the center frame is firmly braced.

Which wall to construct first is a matter of choice. I suspect any sequence you follow will present its own set of problems. I will share what I did; you can adapt my experience to solve your own complications if you choose another sequence. My choices and work process was adapted to the fact that I worked alone much of the time, saving the heaviest and most complex tasks for Saturdays when Greg was available.

If you can muster at least four helpers and preferably six, you should be able to raise an entire wall, but this is tricky. Since a weak point exists where the horizontals connect, I recommend you stay with the half-frame plan, particularly for the long sides. If you want to attempt raising the entire wall structure, strengthen the joint by tying a long board along each side of the horizontal and extending several feet each direction. Pad the beam with paper, cardboard, or cloths to avoid gouges. Even with this added strength, the wall must be hoisted evenly. At least three pulleys are necessary: one toward each end and one in the center at the joint. The guy rope may be tied to a truck, tractor, or similar anchor if no tree or post is available.

If one or more trees are available to the side of the house, the wall frame can be built flat on the sill beams as done with the center framing. Since verticals are set 4 feet apart, some will fall between the floor beams. To support them, place 2 x 4's across the floor beams and shim the rest of the structure to ensure that all parts are level. As before, set the feet of the beams to abut exactly where they will be raised.

If you use your center frame to hoist the wall section, set the feet of the verticals on the sill beam where they will be at their final position and extend the verticals out from the house, supported with blocks stacked and shimmed to the same height as the sill beams.

Your upper horizontals should be replicas of your sill logs, except for the porch-side end. The underlap on that end should be 1/3 the thickness of the beam (as in diagram 9). Otherwise, cut them similarly. The length of your vertical beams will depend on your decision whether to set your floor joists flush with or above the sill beams. If you set the joists on top of the cross beams, as I did, you may want to extend the length of your verticals by the width of the joists, to give you 8' from floor to upper crossbeam, 8' 7 1/2" floor to ceiling. On the other hand, if you plan to use sheetrock or other standard wallboard, a ceiling higher than 8 feet will require patching the outside sheathing. Whatever you decide, be sure you figure your window sills measured up from the finished floor.

Lay the verticals out in their exact places. As before, they will be secured to the sill beam by short iron rods. I used 1/2" rods for the thicker verticals and 3/8" rods for the smaller ones. As with the previous verticals, we used the protruding bolts where they existed; where they did not, we inserted the iron rods into the sill beams; they serve as braces when you raise the frame.

Obviously, your measurements must be carefully made. That is why exact placement is so important. Measure the sill beam for 4-foot centers, beginning at one end, and make a light mark at each point. Either drill your hole dead center on both the vertical and the sill beam or follow some other consistent measurement, such as 2 inches in from each outside surface. Just be sure the verticals will set exactly where you want them. Measure individually for the protruding bolts.

Small pilot holes will help with accurate drilling, and you should drill perhaps a quarter of an inch deeper than the rods to make sure any dust does not keep your beams from seating.

The next step is to attach the verticals to the upper horizontal. Drill the holes to ensure that the outsides of each vertical is flush with upper and lower horizontals. Double check your measurements from each end, upper and lower, to be sure they match. Otherwise, the verticals could be out of plumb sideways. Drill the holes, insert the rods, and pull the verticals tightly onto the upper horizontal.

Window and door openings

The next step in constructing the wall framing is to add 4 x 6 beams crossways between verticals to create the window and door openings. This step is easier to do at this point than later; moreover, the headers and sills will provide strength for the frame as it is raised.

The headers and sills for doors and windows are to be built to the rough opening sizes you have planned. To avoid extra work and material, use a vertical beam for one side of each window and door, leaving only one side to add later.

If your work has gone properly thus far, your wall frames should be square, but this is the time to recheck the alignment of each vertical with both sill and upper beams.

The sills and headers for windows and doors will be attached to the verticals by tongue and groove, cut to the depth of the recess you made to receive siding and wallboard. Measure the distance between verticals from the thick sections. If your structure is square, the sill and header within each section will be identical. Do not assume, though, that each section is exactly the same; treat each separately. Cut your sills and headers to size and cut out the grooves to receive them.

Cut siding recesses in your sills and headers to match those in your verticals. Cut the recesses into opposite sides of the *bottom* of each sill and the *top* of each header. Be sure not to make cuts on the surfaces that will frame the windows or doors.

Place the sills and headers into place and attach them with two 16-penny nails or 3-inch screws, toenailed from the bottom side. Do not depend on the hardware to pull the pieces together completely. If a gap exists at any joint, use clamps to pull and hold the pieces together while you drive in your nails. Use padding to protect the wood.

The slanting verticals I described above (photo 5) may be installed now or later. I chose to do so later just to be certain my walls were plumb when erected, an extra caution perhaps. This process also avoided having the extra weight of the braces as I hoisted the wall.

Once again, paint the exterior exposures with stain preservative before lifting the wall into place. Since there are no angle supports at the corners, tie them securely with hemp rope to provide added strength. Follow the same procedure as described for the center framing. Be sure each vertical is pressed firmly against the rod or bolt it will fit over. Begin the hoisting, observing the precautions described above. About halfway up, tap the verticals so that the holes and rods match up, then complete the hoisting. If you are raising a 16-foot section, one guy rope probably is enough if it is centrally placed. For the 32-foot section, I would not feel safe with less than three.

Again, everyone on your team should be instructed to get out of harm's way as quickly as possible if you begin to lose control. The beams are very strong. They may come apart but they will not break. Better a little time lost for reworking than an injury. Greg and I lifted all of the frames into place by ourselves. Our practice while hoisting was to use ropes long enough that we would not be in danger if we lost control of the frame.

With your helpers maintaining their holds on the ropes, attach temporary braces every eight feet, making sure each vertical is plumb. Have braces ready with at least one nail in each end so they can be attached quickly. Add a second nail in each end when the frame is plumb and secure. The sills and headers do not secure the frame against lateral movement, so if you do not install the long angle braces while the structure is prone, nail temporary lumber braces to run the other way on a slant from at least two verticals to a sill beam.

With the temporary braces in place and the ropes removed, your next task is to install the permanent angle beams if not already done. These are set inside the four-foot sections and will not show after your siding is installed. They can be rough on their upper and lower sides but must be the same thickness as the inset section of the verticals: If a vertical is 5 1/2 inches deep, minus a one-inch recess on each side, the braces must be 3 1/2 inches thick.

If you can assemble enough helpers to raise this long wall in one full section, you are ready at this point to begin another section. If your manpower is limited as mine was to two men--myself and Greg--you should construct and hoist half the wall, then build the other half one beam at a time. The half you

49

6

choose to hoist should be the heaviest and most awkward one, probably the side with the most doors and windows.

The process for the remaining partial wall is a combination of steps already described. Set your beams on the work surface just as if you are going to build it for hoisting. Carefully mark and drill holes for the protruding bolts and steel rods, and insert the rods in both ends of the beams. You will not assemble the structure, of course, since you will lift the beams individually. The procedure is basically the same as described for the second half of the center beam structure.

Temporarily fit all verticals that will contain door or window framing onto the upper horizontal by slipping the rods into their holes. Once the verticals are squared, they will be spaced properly for you to prepare headers, sills, and grooves for them. When all components are cut, you may lift them into place one at a time or wrestle a combined window or door section in one piece. If you do the latter, permanently attach the headers and sills. Lifting the combined pieces is not as difficult as it sounds if the section consists of only two verticals. You will butt the feet of the verticals against rods or bolts and lift the structure into place with much of the weight resting on the sill beam. I followed this procedure because I prefer to do everything I can on the ground. If you raise one component at a time, raise the verticals, secure them, and tap the sills and headers into place with a wood mallet.

For this second section of a wall, you should erect the corner beam first. Seat it over the protruding bolt, plumb it, and brace it well with temporary braces. Next, tie a long board near the top of this corner beam and to the nearest vertical of the raised half of the wall. You will tie the other verticals to this board as you raise them rather than brace them individually (photo 6). The ropes leave enough play to allow you to maneuver the rods into their holes when you raise the upper horizontal.

You will lift the upper horizontal into place in the same way as the center horizontal. The singular difference is that you have more verticals onto which to fit it. This makes the task more difficult and more dangerous. Greg and I managed this together, but it really is a three-person job, one on each end of the upper horizontal and one maneuvering the pins of the verticals into their holes.

Greg and I handled the task by tying the connecting end of the upper beam into place, then tying the other end more loosely. We wanted the second end to be maneuverable but safe in case it was dropped. Greg, who is stronger than I am, tied a ladder outside the corner vertical so he could move the beam as necessary while I lined up the holes

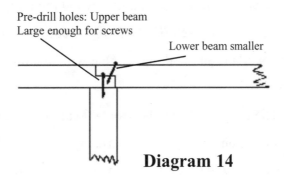

Pre-drill holes: Upper beam
Large enough for screws

Lower beam smaller

Diagram 14

from below.

With all the pins well seated, we were ready to secure the ends of the two horizontals where they overlapped. We drilled holes to receive large bolts (diagram 14). Predrill the holes: a larger hole through the beam to be attached, a smaller hole through the beam to which it is attached. This finished securing the structure. The addition of the long angle beams completed the wall.

Other wall frames

I chose to assemble the back wall next, the end opposite where the porch would be. The south wall (diagram 11) contains two small windows for the bath and kitchen, one in each of the 12' sections.

The two sections of this wall must be built individually. The wall cannot be built first and then hoisted because of the interference of vertical beams already in place. As you can see from diagram 10, each side has only two verticals between the corner beam and the center beam. The window sill and header connects the two verticals. Again, I constructed and raised these into place as units, then braced them securely. The last vertical to be raised was the opposite corner beam which would tie into the other long wall.

The upper horizontal is in two sections, each 12' 3" long; the extra 3 inches on each beam is to continue beyond the midpoint by 3 inches each way, making the overlap itself 6". Before you cut, be sure to think through which ends are overlaps and underlaps. One will be a mid-point lap, the other an overlap.

The corners of each horizontal beam is cut to overlap the already raised wall frame on one end and to underlap the not-yet-raised wall at the other end. These two horizontals are secured with long screws as before.

I felt a real sense of exhiliration when this wall was complete. , *Gosh,* I thought, *I can actually do this stuff*! We blessed the event with a family picnic.

The other long wall (diagram 13) is constructed the same as the previous one. Put the free half together prone and hoist it into place, then construct the connecting section one beam at a time. With this frame complete, the feeling of accomplishment just keeps getting better.

The porch-side wall frame (north, diagram 10) contains four verticals, in addition to the corners already in place. The windowed half is put together and erected as was the south wall, except that for aesthetic reasons I decided to inset the frame one inch from the corners and center post, rather than make them flush.

At each upper corner of this section, three beams interconnect (east and west wall beams respectively, north wall beam, and porch beam). They overlap in 1/3 cuts. I added the porch beam after completing the wall frame.

Recall the discussion about building the center frame, the first set of verticals constructed. The upper center porch beam referenced there is added at this point. As discussed, the underlap of the center horizontal measures 3 3/4" deep x 3 3/4" thick by the full width of the beam. The connecting porch beam abuts the center beam and continues in a straight line. The transverse wall beams coming the other way butt against each other at the midpoint of the center vertical (diagram 15).

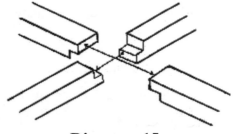

Diagram 15

Since the porch beam is added later, when you attach the upper horizontal wall beams a sort of mortise will be left into which the tenon of the porch beam will be inserted. Be sure to keep the mortise clear of screws or nails.

The other half of the north wall, with the patio door, requires a different approach. I constructed the opening for a 6-foot sliding door (photo 7). Its outside frame is the 8 x 8 corner vertical beam. The inside frame is a 6 x 6 vertical; the size is both for strength and aesthetics. It is the only additional vertical beam in this section. Before I raised this vertical, I cut a groove to receive a header beam for the sliding door. It is the same depth by 4 1/2 inches thick. A corresponding mortise has to be cut into the 8 x 8 corner post, inset 1" on each side. With sufficient care, a circular saw may be used to begin this cut. Set the blade to the proper depth and cut carefully along your lines, then cut kerfs of the same depth between the lines to make the chisel work easier.

7

Square the corners of the cut with a chisel where the sawblade left a rounded portion. If you do not square the corners first, before cleaning out the mortise, you may split the one-inch border. (If you are sure of your measurements, you can prepare this mortise earlier before raising the corner post.) Be very careful using a circular saw above your head. For safety, stand on a ladder so you are above your work. Don't ever use such a dangerous tool unless your position allows you complete control and leverage.

Raise the 6 x 6 vertical beam into place, with the rods set properly in the bottom and top. Make certain it is plumb and brace it securely. Next, measure the length needed for the sliding door header. Cut recesses into the top side of the header, inside and out, to receive the siding and interior treatment just as with

54

the window and door headers. An upper horizontal will span the header too close to allow room to work between them. Before you fix it into place, determine the portion of it that will be directly over this header and nail a 2 x 4 onto its bottom side to provide a surface onto which to nail siding and sheetrock.

You will not have enough space to secure the header from above. Toenail it on the sides with 16-penny nails or 3-inch screws, countersunk, placing your fasteners so they will be covered with door trim.

With the verticals in place, the next step is to raise each of the upper horizontals, using the same technique as before. Secure the ends with large screw bolts. Attach the diagonal braces; my design has one between the window and the corner and another longer one between the 8 x 8 center post and the 6 x 6 vertical.

Framing for the porch is next. Three 6 x 6 verticals, three 6 x 8 horizontals tied into the wall frame, and two 6 x 8 spans between the outer verticals are required. This frame is put together just as the rest of the house, but simpler because there are no intermediate verticals or diagonal braces within each span.

There is not enough room on the sill beams to work on the porch framing. The structure can be constructed flat if there are no obstructions on the porch side of the house, following the procedure described for the first wall frame. If trees or other obstructions exist on that side, the beams have to be raised individually.

If you construct the framing flat, affix the steel rods into the verticals, then attach the two upper horizontals that connect the verticals. The outer ends of the horizontals are notched for an underlap to receive the connecting beams. The center ends of the two horizontals do not overlap but butt together over the center post. However, they are integrated into the connecting beam so must be notched. In photo 8, notice that the connecting beam—which runs from the house to the outer vertical beam—sets directly on top of the vertical beam. It has a one-half thickness underlap, over which the two 12' outer spans are fitted, with their ends butted together. If you raise the outer section, reverse the overlap and underlap. You also can construct this joint by using one-third overlaps as discussed with the back (kitchen and bath) wall.

If you erect the beams individually, insert the rods into the verticals and raise them to be flush at the corners and sides of the sill logs. The two horizontals that complete the outside of the porch are 12 feet long and heavy, while the three connecting horizontals are 8 feet long. The shorter ones should be raised first. Predrill holes through the overlap of each beam to receive screw bolts.

If you are working alone, lift the end first that attaches to the house and secure it with rope (diagram 16). Be sure to place your ladder so that if you drop the beam it will not fall on you or the ladder.

Attach a ladder to the secured vertical of the porch. With the rope tied to the other end of the beam, raise this end carefully until you can get a safe grip on it. Set the overlap flush into place, insert a screw bolt through the hole and strike it with a hammer enough to get it started. Do not screw it into place yet. Tie the joint with rope, then move back to the other end of the beam. With a long bit, drill a hole into the underlap to receive the screw bolt and screw it firmly into place. Move back to the porch end, check to be sure the overlap is aligned, drill a smaller hole in the underlap, and screw it into place.

Repeat this procedure with the other two beams that span the porch. Slip the center beam into its "mortise" and run a 10" bolt all the way through from the top beam, the porch beam, and into the vertical. The two long horizontals are raised the same way, one end at a time. They are half again heavier and their length adds to their being unwieldy. The safest course is to wait until you have a helper. If you must work alone, be sure to think through every possible accident that could happen. Make sure your ladder is secure and out of harm's way. Always drop your work rather than take a chance on falling or suffering a muscle injury.

At this point the porch framing is in place but is not secure against lateral movement. Since long diagonal braces are not reasonable here, corner braces must be added. I made these exactly like the ones for the center frame (photo 8). I used four, one at each end and two for the center.

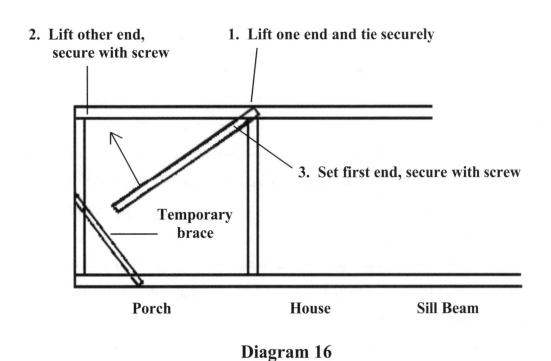

2. Lift other end, secure with screw

1. Lift one end and tie securely

3. Set first end, secure with screw

Temporary brace

Porch   **House**   **Sill Beam**

Diagram 16

Cross beams

Your house is taking shape beautifully, but the first floor framing is not yet complete. Horizontal beams must be raised into place to connect the outer walls to the center beams, one every eight feet (3 beams down each long wall, diagram 17). These beams are fastened just as are the floor beams, with some

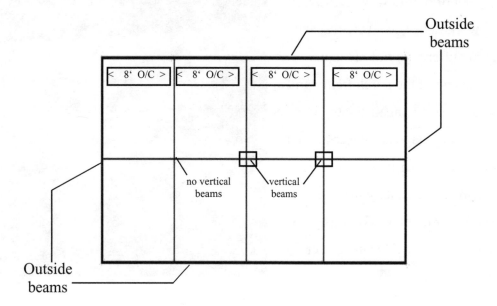

Diagram 17

variation of a mortise-and-tenon joint.

These cross beams serve two structural purposes. First, they tie the outer walls together to keep them from bowing out over time. Second, they support any upper floor you add. The mortise and tenon cuts do not weaken the beams too much, so long as you plan well for how you cut them. Removing wood from the thickness rather than the width is important. Cut your tenons to two-thirds the thickness of the beam. Wood is much stronger top to bottom than side to side. In other words, a 4 x 8 is much stronger than a square beam with the same amount of wood (a little larger than a 5 x 6). Thus, a thicker rather than a wider tenon makes a stronger beam.

Think through the relative strength of each joint. The upper horizontals of the wall frame are well braced, their weight and that of the roof transferred to the foundation piers by the long diagonal braces. The 8 x 8 vertical beam in the center of the house supports upper beams that come from each direction, 1" of its surface available on each side for crossbeams. This will be your strongest crossbeam joint. The 6 x 6 vertical beam to the right (diagram 4) provides adequate support for an upper floor. The upper horizontal to the left of the center beam spans sixteen feet with no intermediate support. Obviously, this is the weakest crossbeam joint.

If you do not plan to put a second floor over this area, the mortise-and-tenon joint is strong enough. If you plan a second floor, I would not recommend cutting into the center horizontal to attach crossbeams. Use a metal joist hanger of the sort used for 4 x 4 posts, trimming the beam end to this dimension. Plan to run your floor joists across the 12' span, from outside wall to center beam. The other option is to add a vertical beam under the horizontal at this point, if it does not interfere too greatly with your plans for the first floor. If you plan to break this open space into two or more rooms, the vertical post may be a good choice.

I cut the mortises and tenons at this stage, the tenons before I raised the beams. I set the beams in place, marked for the mortises, pushed the crossbeam aside, cut the mortise, and dropped the crossbeam into place, all the work done on a ladder. The crossbeams are almost twelve feet in length. Raise them the same way you raised the porch horizontals; they are about the same weight. When the crossbeams are in place, secure each joint with a barn nail.

Attach angle braces at each end of the two central crossbeams, the beams that meet over the 8 x 8 vertical in the center of the house (photo 4). The framing for your first story is finished. Party time.

Chapter 4

Framing the Second Story

Consider the Options

The first story frame is strong enough to support a full second story. Several design options are possible. First, determine how much floor space you want. Beds sometimes can fit against a knee wall, but you want an 8-foot ceiling in the walk space. Make a scale drawing, using diagrams 18--21 as a starting point. Try out several pitches to decide which best fits your needs.

The pitch of the roof makes a lot of difference for both floor space and appearance. Remember that high-pitched roofs shed snow and ice better than low-sloped roofs. In warmer climates, a lower pitch is sufficient. Flat roofs are not recommended; they almost always develop leaks unless commercial in design. A high-pitched roof allows space in the center for second-story rooms, sometimes with knee walls to expand the useable space. For full second floors, the roof will be planned much as for a single story home. Obviously, the roof style is part of any decision about the second story.

For one- or two-story houses, a quarter-pitch roof is a good choice in warm to moderate climates; that is, the pitch rises three inches for every horizontal foot. To determine the length of rafters needed (diagram 18), draw a

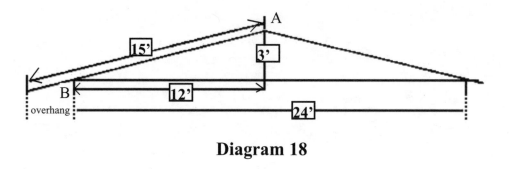

Diagram 18

line to scale to represent the top horizontal beam of a gable end of your house. If your plans follow mine, this line will represent 24 feet. At the midpoint, draw a perpendicular line to represent the height you want for the gable. The top of this line represents the point of the ridge. For a quarter pitch, this line will be 36 inches (3" per foot). Draw a line from the ridge to the outside wall and carry the line over at least one foot for overhang. Measure the sloping line. Apply your scale; this is the length you will need for rafters. If you want enough height in the attic for storage, your pitch will have to be higher. For second-story space with knee walls, the pitch will be much higher.

Here are five design options for a second story:

Option 1: Full story with eight-foot walls. With this design, you will construct the walls of the second story essentially the same as the first story. The verticals will rise directly above the verticals below, held in place by pins and using angle braces as described above. The roof likely will be a lower pitch than in the other options, but you can choose any slope.

Option 2: Knee-wall plus high-pitched roof (diagram 19). In this design, you will raise four-foot walls, plus or minus, on top of your first floor horizontals.

62

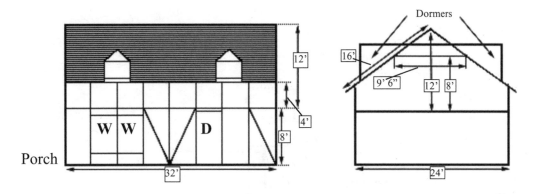

Diagram 19

To carry the weight of the roof, you will use the "king pole" construction, explained in the chapter on roofs. You may want dormers so as to have windows in the long walls. I have not discussed dormers in this book, since I have not built any, but you will have no trouble finding a book that describes this process.

Option 3: Full-length high-pitched roof (diagram 20). This plan has the roof rafters resting on the first-story beams. The pitch must be severe in order to allow sufficient space on the second floor. To determine your approximate floor space, draw a line to scale representing half of one end of the house (diagram 20); in my design, this would represent 12 feet. The 16' and 24' marks represent wider house plans. These would require different construction methods for support. Draw a perpendicular line at one end to represent your rise at the ridgeline. It will need to be at least 12' and as much as 18' high. Draw lines from the 12-foot point of the horizontal line to each one foot point of the vertical line, beginning at 12'.

Using your scale, mark on each increment where the roof line will be eight feet from the floor. Note that the slope from the 12-foot mark provides four feet of 8-foot ceiling. Doubled for the full gable width, you have eight feet of full-height floor space for your second floor. If you measure the rafter length, you find the slope requires a 17' rafter, plus overhang, about 18'6" total. If you carry the 8' ceiling to the 14' increment, you will have a little over 5 feet per side,

63

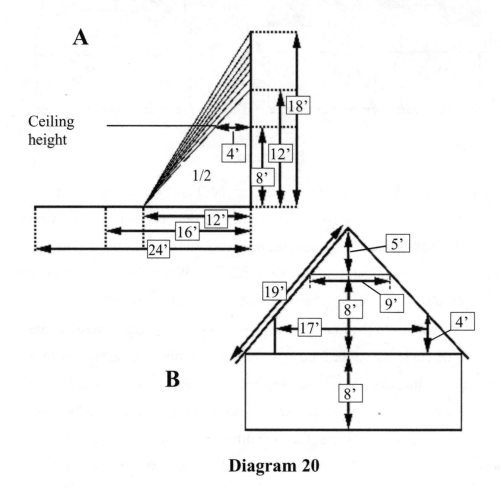

A

Ceiling
height

18'

4'

12'

1/2

8'

12'

16'

24'

B

5'

19'

8'

9'

17'

4'

8'

Diagram 20

doubled to10 feet of width. This height requires 18'6" rafters, plus overhang, about 20' total. Make a preliminary choice, then draw floor plans to include whatever you want on the second floor, such as two bedrooms and a bath, to be sure you can do what you want with the available space. Don't forget to allow space for a stairway.

Option 4: Full-length barn-style upper story (diagram 21). This style allows the use of shorter lengths of lumber due to construction methods. Apart from the gable ends, the entire second story, both roof and walls, will be covered

64

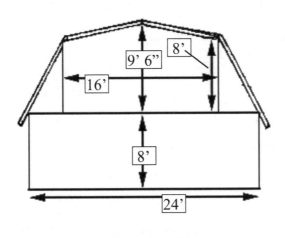

Diagram 21

with roofing. If you want windows on the sides, they will be dormers, shallow ones due to the steep pitch. Skylights set into the upper portion of the barn roof are a good option. The ridge may be higher than in the diagram if you desire more pitch. The elbow angle may be adjusted as desired, which will affect headroom. This process is described later. To determine the available floor space, draw scales as described above.

Option 5: The design I selected is a story-and-a-half combination. The first story is a 4/12 slope (4" rise per foot) to form an open beam cathedral ceiling over half the house. The second story uses the barn roof design, built over the other half of the structure (photo 1). This is the method I describe below. My choice was based solely on available stock.

As things turned out, I like it very much for our intended use of the house. As a house to live in, it would require modification. Two bedrooms can be added easily, one upstairs and one downstairs, by extending the barn roof to add a wing on the west side of the house, the side shown in the photo. The door shown and the window above it can be doors from the halls into the bedrooms. In both cases, each new bedroom would be located next to a bathroom.

The second story floor

I ran 2 x 12 floor joists across the 12-foot span. I could have run 2 x 8s the other direction onto the connecting beams (diagram 17). Since I am neither engineer nor architect, I chose the strongest structural option. This choice created minor problems later in running the plumbing.

I set my joists one inch in from the outside beam to allow room for siding. The two joists butt together on top of the center horizontal. If you square your center horizontal beam, the operation is straightforward. If you leave the top of the horizontal beam rounded when you construct it as I did, you will need to cut out level spaces for the joists to fit. I did this with a chain saw and smoothed the cut with a chisel. It would have been quicker in the long run to square the beam on all sides.

Floors tend to squeak after use. To avoid this annoyance, braces should be set between the joists. Inexpensive metal straps are available for this purpose. I used them on the top floor, three per joist. When I built the lower floor later, though, I went back to the old-fashioned method. It seems much more secure to me. These are simply wood angle braces set in an X pattern from the top of one joist to the bottom of the next. Set the two pieces of the X together between each joist and run them from joist to joist in a straight line. The wood braces have the added advantage of forcing into alignment any joists that are slightly bowed or twisted. I attached them with 2 1/2" all-purpose screws.

Do not take chances working on the second story by trying to balance on floor joists. It is best to build a floor, but if you are in an area where rain is frequent and your floor will be exposed for more than a few days, you will have to protect the floor or, as I did, use scrap plywood sheets.

Since we receive considerable rain in Tennessee, Greg located some used 1/2" plywood at a cheap price. We laid the pieces across the joists for a temporary floor. This gave us the safety without having to worry about the plywood being ruined. When I did heavy lifting, I doubled the plywood where I was working. If you live in a dry climate or plan to work fast, you can go ahead and lay the floor. Plywood should be 3/4" for floors. Pressboard supposedly is as strong or stronger than plywood of the same dimensions and is considerably cheaper, but pressboard swells when it soaks up water. I did not want to contend with that in the building process or later if a roof or commode leak were to develop.

Planning the barn style rafters

I worked on a design for the walls and ceiling of this second floor barn style a good while, trying out different angles of cuts for the roof and sides. Different angles obviously result in different amounts of floor space available.

The barn joist consists of two pieces of lumber joined together at an elbow to create your desired angle. Obviously, the elbow is the weak point in the rafter and must be strengthened. This is done with short lengths of 1 x 6s laid across the two boards (diagram 22). You must carefully plan the dimensions of your roof. Several factors are involved: How high must your ridgeline be to allow adequate interior space? What slope do you want on the upper part of the roof? What angle is best at the elbow? What lengths must be cut so that the upper part of the rafter will rest on the ridgepole and the lower part on the horizontal beam?

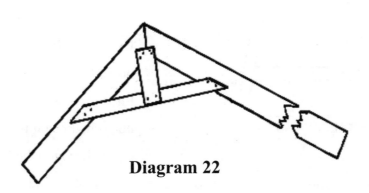

Diagram 22

The best way to determine your design is to begin by drawing several examples to scale. Once you have a general idea of what will provide the floor space you want and the general appearance that you want externally, then you should lay our pieces out on a flat area such as a driveway. If no flat area is available, use wood planks or beams to level your pieces as you work. This step is tedious but necessary. Cut a short piece and a long piece, each a couple of feet longer than you think you may use for your joists, including overhang (diagram

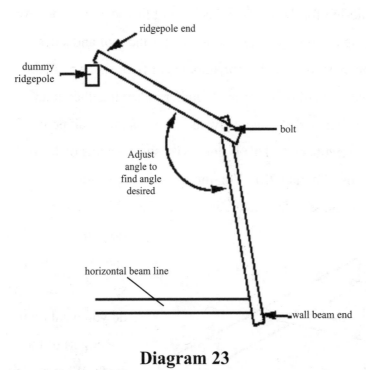

Diagram 23

23). I used 2 x 6s, but 1 x 6s will work as well for a model and are lighter to maneuver. Bolt a long piece and a short piece together at one end, leaving them loose enough for the angle to be adjusted. Use a chalkline or board to establish a line to represent the horizontal beam for one-half your gable width. The bottom of the rafter will rest on the outside end . The other end represents the gable centerpoint, below the ridge. Next, set an object, one heavy enough that it will not shift, at the point to represent your ridge. Its corner should be directly above the gable side of the lower line. Set it at the height you anticipate your ridgepole to be. The barn rafter will rest on the corner of this object, so position it exactly.

68

Working with these two fixed points, the ridgepole and the wall line, maneuver the hinged rafter until you are satisfied with the floor space. You will notice that when you push the upper arm higher onto the ridgepole, the headroom decreases. You may, of course, raise or lower the ridgepole to change the angle. As you adjust the boards to various angles, you will notice that the wider the angle, the longer the boards must be and the more floor space and headroom is available; sharper angles shorten the board lengths and also lessen the space, but may be advisable if you receive heavy snows. On the other hand, the upper arm—which represents the flattest part of the roof—represents a fairly small roof portion, so snow load should not be a problem in most localities.

When you have made your decision, run a couple of screws through the elbow to keep it from shifting, then store it in a safe place. Do not make any cuts on it at this time. Measure for the height of your ridgepole from the horizontal beam line. Constructing and raising the ridgepole is your next step.

The ridgepole assembly

The ridgepole assembly is much like the center beam structure of the first floor. It consists of five pieces: three vertical beams to support two horizontals that meet over the center vertical. You also need four corner braces. The length of the verticals are determined by the height you want the ridgepole to be. Each ridgepole beam, in my case, was 13'3" long. The horizontal beam(s) overlap the outer verticals 1 foot, to provide for roof overhang. The extra 3" is to provide for a 6" overlap of the two beams at the center, as in previous fittings.

The vertical beams that support the ridgepole are "king poles." If you examine several barns, you will find that some are built without vertical supports. The rafters butt against a board that forms the ridge. In this construction all the weight is carried by the walls. The king pole structure reverses the weight, transferring it to the supports below. In our case, each vertical beam rests directly above another one which in turn rests on a concrete pier. Because the ridge cannot sag, the lower ends of the rafters press inward rather than outward on the wall.   Either structure will work, but I have seen a barns with wavy wall lines. I prefer the king pole structure.

To assemble the structure, follow the same procedures as before. Construct the assembly flat, in this case on the floor of the second story. As before, set the foot of each vertical at the rod it will seat over. The rods that hold the horizontals to the verticals are not strong enough alone. Predrill holes and run long screw bolts through the horizontals at each point they connect to the verticals. If two 12-foot lengths are used for the horizontal, one screw bolt can be run through the overlap onto the center vertical, then another one through the joining overlap into the first (diagram 14). Angle braces should be attached to each joint, one to each end vertical and two to the center vertical.

With the structure complete, be sure the feet are positioned properly. The very heavy structure is raised in one piece. If a tall tree is accessible, set a pulley high enough for proper leverage. It should be almost as high as the structure will be when upright, somewhat higher if possible, and as nearly centered to the structure as possible. Be sure to attach guy ropes to keep from pulling the structure too far and losing control of it.

You likely will have the same problem I did. A tree was accessible but an adequate limb was not high enough for proper leverage. Placing the pulley lower causes the line of pull to be too low. To raise the structure, the line of pull must be fairly close to the imaginary line the horizontal will follow when raised.

The only solution in this situation is to manhandle the structure. I placed the pulley as high as possible by climbing a ladder set against a nearby tree and throwing a large bolt attached to a cord across a high limb. The cord was attached to a rope which held the pulley. I pulled it into place and secured the rope. I figured the lower line of pull would be adequate once the structure was partly raised.

Three men can manhandle the structure without too much trouble, one at each joint. I worked alone on this part of the project, so it took me a while to finish it. Round up several blocks and set them on the upper horizontals so as to be easily reached as you work with the ridgepole. Lift one end a foot or so and place a block under it. Move to the center and repeat the process, then again at the other end. Repeat this procedure to block up the structure another foot or so. Instruct your helpers not to take chances. Be sure they stay outside the line of danger if the structure falls off the blocks.

Raise the structure by placing a block under each joint one at a time. Begin with longer blocks. After I raised the structure three feet or so, I was able to raise it the rest of the way by winch. The height of the necessary manhandling will vary depending on how high your pulley is. When the structure is raised about midpoint, check the holes at the feet to be sure they are in line with the pins. Complete the raising, plumb the structure, and secure it with temporary braces.

The next step is to build your rafters, but some planning steps are necessary. First, establish 24" centers down the upper wall beam to indicate where the butts of the rafters will be set. Begin above the lower horizontal beam, not at the end of the overhang. Then make corresponding inline marks on the ridgepole.

Now is the time to retrieve your rafter model from storage. Place it on a corresponding set of ridgepole and wall beam marks and secure it temporarily, or have a helper hold it in place. Use a carpenter's square to mark the notch that will rest on the ridgepole. Repeat the process at the horizontal beam.

The rafters should be notched at the ridgepole in such dimensions that they touch their opposites, and deep enough at the wall beam so the wall will carry their weight rather than depend on nails to hold them into place. The square will give you the proper angle, but you may have to adjust the lines to bring your rafter to midpoint on the spine of the ridgepole. Make a too-shallow cut and work up to the depth you want, and be sure to make upper and lower cuts together.

When you have the fit you want, place the model rafter at several points to check consistency. Do not assume all your cuts will be the same. If your ridgepole or wall beams are off slightly, you will have to adjust your cuts. Slight variations must be dealt with during the assembly of your rafters. Make a chart to record the differences. If they are all the same or only fractionally different, you are of all people must blessed. Don't worry about the overhang at this point.

Build and install the barn rafters

After all this preparation, you are ready to begin putting your rafters together. Each rafter has six parts, four of which are for reinforcement: the two long extensions of the rafter, two cross braces of about 36", and two small plywood stabilizers (photo 9, diagram 22).

The first step is to assemble the two rafter lengths. The model has the pieces overlapping at the elbow. For the actual rafter, the pieces butt together at the elbow, so each piece must be cut the to appropriate angle. You can determine the angles from the model. One way to do this is to saw through both thicknesses.

Cut the short and long boards to pattern and arrange the pieces to form the elbow. Fasten them by running a long screw through an edge; this will pull them together. Next, attach the cross braces (at least 36") with 1 ½" - 2" screws, one cross brace on each side. You may cut them all the same length even if the joist measurements vary slightly, but they must be placed onto every rafter in the same position each time. This precision is necessary because the cross braces will provide the surface onto which to attach the interior wall treatment. You may want to cut the ends on an angle to provide more surface for screws.

9

Last, reinforce the elbow with 1/4-inch plywood about 3 inches wide; these run from the elbow to the cross brace on each side. If your prior measurements indicate your rafters must vary a bit to set on the ridgepole and horizontal beam, lay these small braces aside until the ridgepole is in place. You may have to modify the angle slightly. If your measurements from wall beam to ridgepole are the same at each two-foot increment, your rafters can be identical; otherwise, modify each one as you go. Slight adjustments can be made without recutting by loosening the screws on one end of the cross braces, dropping the rafter into place, and resetting the screws.

With the rafters put together, you are ready to lift them into place. They are heavy and unwieldy; two men are required to handle them safely. I pulled mine up with rope. If you have a third helper, he or she can attach the rope to the rafters from the ground. Raise one rafter into place and check the fit of the notches at the ridgepole and the wall beam. Adjust if necessary. Allow a foot or so for overhang, though the steepness of the barn style will result in an eave of only six or seven inches.

It is not structurally essential for opposite rafters that rest on the ridgepole to touch; however, if they are off much your roof line will not be right. The strongest joint will be if the bottoms of the notches rest flat on their surfaces.

The rafters at each end of the ridge are constructed differently in order to provide a strong overhang. These will be installed later. The first rafters to be positioned are two feet in, on center, from the tip of each ridgepole end, and also the ones in the center. (In photo 9, my ridgepole is longer than the overhang I decided on. I cut the excess off later.) Set the rafters on both sides of the ridgepole; this will secure it firmly. Drive a barn nail through each rafter at the horizontal beam and at the ridgepole. Barn nails secure a structure well enough to withstand a very strong wind.

If you are following my design, the rafters that face the interior of the house do not overhang (see photo 9, left side). They must be trimmed. Secure this rafter onto the ridgepole with a barn nail, then set its notch properly onto the first-story crossbeam. Toenail a small nail into its side, so placing it as not to interfere with the cut I am about to describe. Hold a square against the horizontal beam and up the rafter surface. Mark for a cut rising up flush with the beam. Once the cut is made, you can secure the rafter with a barn nail.

A hint for later: The interior wall treatment (e.g. sheetrock) will be attached above the beam to the rafter surface left from this cut. If the cut is flush with the beam as described, the raw edge of your wall treatment will be exposed and will require trim over it. To avoid the need for trim, you may want your interior wallboard to rest on the top of the beam. If so, make your vertical cut on the rafter to accommodate the thickness of the wallboard, leaving a ½" or so ledge on the beam.

You must brace each rafter as you raise it. Their shape and weight will cause them to tip over if they are not secured.   Use long 1 x 4s running from the ridgepole to the upper part of the rafter near the elbow to secure them

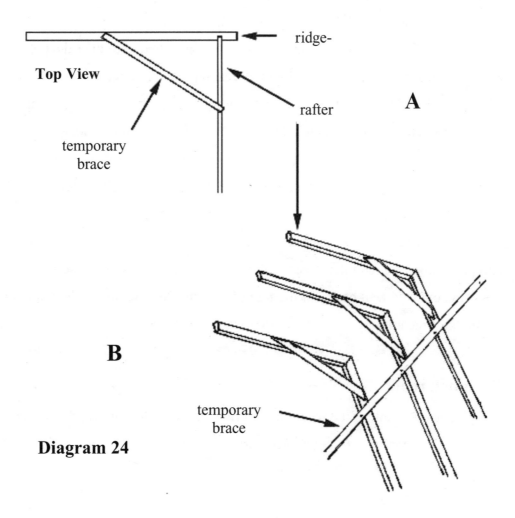

Top View

ridge-

rafter

A

temporary
brace

B

temporary
brace

Diagram 24

75

temporarily (diagram 24A). After you raise the two end and center rafters, you can nail a board horizontally just under the angle braces (diagram 24B). Make sure your already-raised rafters are plumb, then attach this brace. Mark 24" centers onto the temporary brace. As you raise succeeding rafters into place, they in turn will be fastened to this brace at the 24" center marks. Leave all braces in place until the decking is placed on the roof.

When all the rafters are in place, you are ready to prepare "ladders" for each gable end. This assembly essentially is comprised of two rafters like your previous ones, fastened together by short 2 x 6 or 2 x 8 "rungs" (photo 9). My rafters are 2 x 8s; I used 2 x 6 rungs to leave room for the eave enclosure to be inset between the rafters.

The inside rafter of the ladder assembly is installed onto the ridgepole and wall beam just as the others. The foot will rest on the horizontal beam. The top of the outside rafter rests on the eave extension of the ridgepole; its foot hangs loose at the bottom. Do not notch this foot. Nail the rungs of the ladder on 24" centers. The ladder construction provides strength for the overhang; some carpenters add an additional ladder arrangement to the next set of rafters as well for additional strength.

This structure is very heavy and requires careful handling. I raised these into place alone, which I don't recommend. If you must work alone, screw a 2 x 4 extension onto the wall beam for the foot of the outside rafter to rest on until you secure the structure.

The pitch roof

The other half of the roof runs at a right angle to the barn roof, is lower, and is of a different construction. This structure is much easier than the barn style but requires a careful tie-in where the two roofs come together.

As before, the ridgepole is raised first. My design called for 4' king poles. I set three of them. One is over the center post where the porch joins the house (photo 7), another is halfway down the open beam and so has no vertical support beneath it (photo 10, shown after sheetrock applied), and the last is above the pole in the center of the house. This last one intrudes into the barn roof. Set these in place with steel rods and secure them with temporary braces. Before you lift them into place, drill the top of each king pole dead center for 3/8" rods.

Two 6 x 8 horizontals are required for the ridgepole, a 16' one to span the living area and an 8' one to span the porch. Double-check your measurements to determine the exact lengths. Cut 6" half-laps to join the two beams together. The far ends rest on the verticals with no cuts. Drill companion holes for the rods inserted in the king poles, measuring them carefully to ensure the king poles remain plumb when they seat on the rods. After you have the ridgepole in place, long screws can be run through it into the king pole, or toenailed. If toenailed, countersink the holes to fill later. Except for the joint at the barn roof, the structure will be exposed as part of the cathedral ceiling.

The barn end should be secured by nailing or screwing it to one of the barn joists. Plumb the king pole and measure the nearest distance between it and a joist. Cut a block of wood to fill the space, nail or screw it to the joist, and nail or screw the king post to the block.

With the ridgepole in place, you are ready to install the rafters. Unless you can get a carpenter to show you how to use a square to draw angles for rafter cuts, the easiest way to determine your cuts for these straight rafters is for you and a helper to hold a board against the corner of the house on the porch side and trace the angles onto the board. If you work alone, screw one end approximately where it should be, lift and screw the other end, then adjust the first end. Adjust the rafter until you have the angle you want and mark the board. Leave at least a one-foot overhang. Lower the board and make the cuts on the model, then check it at several points along each side. Mark the wall beams and ridgepole at 24" centers. (Remember to start your measurements on the outside edge of the end rafter.) If the rafter does not fit at any point, make notes for whatever adjustments need to be made in your cuts. Remember that the upper and lower cuts must be the same angles, so measure the rafter accordingly. In other words, do not seat one end and not the other; this will change your angle.

The structure of these rafters is straightforward until you come to the barn roof. At that point, your last rafter will be attached to the barn roof. To make sure it is on a level with the other rafters, run a straightedge across the rafters at the lower end and butt it against a barn rafter. Mark that point to indicate where the bottom of the last rafter should be nailed. Attach the top of this rafter to the ridgepole and nail the bottom at the mark. It is possible you will have a slight dogleg where you trimmed the barn rafters to receive interior wall board, or the distance between the bottoms of the last two rafters may exceed 24". If so, attach a shorter fill-in rafter; be sure to extend it to match the overhang. I was afraid laying the valley would be difficult with this angle change, but it proved not to be a problem.

Your structure is ready to roof. Glory!

Chapter 5

Applying the Roof Decking

and Roof

Applying the deck

Roof decking is one of your simplest construction tasks, apart from the fact that every piece is heavy. One-half inch plywood or comparable pressboard is generally used. With 24" inch centers, you might want to add clips between each rafter, available at building supply stores; they are double clips that fit over and under adjoining plywood pieces, applied between rafters to add strength.

The decking should be laid laterally and each run should be staggered. Start at the eave and work up. This way each run can rest on the edge of the one below it. The lowest run begins at a corner. For the next run, cut a 4 x 8 sheet into two 4 x 4s and start it with one of these halves. This way, your joints will be staggered and the roof will be stronger. Place a nail every 4 inches or so at the edges of each piece, every 8 inches or so in between.

To lay the decking is simply a process of laying pieces next to one another until you come to where the roofs join. To fit the decking where roofs join, measure the high and low points from the roof angle back to the decking and transfer the measurements onto the plywood to be cut. An alternate way to determine the angle is to temporarily secure a full sheet in line with the run. Place another sheet against the adjoining roof to follow its angle, with its opposite side overlapping the sheet that is temporarily secured. Mark along the edge to establish the proper angle. Cut the sheet at the mark; the sheet should fall into place.

When you arrive near the ridge, you have a decision to make. Roof space must be ventilated, whether an attic or only space between rafters. If it is not, condensation will cause your eaves and rafters to rot. You may purchase a metal ventilation cap that runs the length of the ridge. You install it along with the roofing at the ridgeline, following the manufacturer's instructions. If you plan an attic, vents are also be installed at the top of the gables and in the eaves. Many builders in the past have installed only the eave and gable vents; the ridgeline vent provides added air flow, thus keeping the attic cooler. This combination allows air to enter through the gable vents and out through the ridge vents.

For a cathedral ceiling, the gable vents are eliminated. The ridgeline vent plus eave vents provides the best ventilation. If you choose not to use the ridgeline vent, fairly adequate ventilation is provided if air can pass freely under the roof decking from one eave to the opposite side. This is the method I chose to use, but if I had it to do over I would use both. The flow-through works this way (for a cathedral ceiling): Insulation is attached later to the bottom of the rafters, allowing about two inches of air-flow space above the insulation. For example, if you want to use 6" batts, use 2 x 8s for rafters. Vents are included in the eave enclosures, which allows air to travel up the rafters on one side and down the other. Obviously, there must be no obstruction at the ridge line.

Installing the roofing

With the decking complete, you are ready to lay the roofing. I will give general instructions, but if you have unusual circumstances you should consult a roofing manual or chapter in a construction book. If your ridgeline is straight with no intersections, the roofing is easy apart from interruptions such as chimneys.

Preparation

The first step is to apply drip edge along the roof edges. This step is especially important along the eaves, but as inexpensive as the material is, I recommend you apply it along the rakes (upslope edges) as well. The drip edge is a thin piece of angled metal, one edge of which has a lip. When nailed onto the roof edge, the half with the lip laps over the side. The lip extends outward to throw water away from the facing. This reduces both rot and frequency of painting.

The next step is to apply any necessary flashing. If you have a straight roof, no flashing is used. If you have a roof that joins to another one, a valley is created on each side of the ridge; these must be flashed. A dormer creates two small valleys; they must be flashed as well. The flashing generally used is aluminum, which can be purchased cut to the proper width. Cut the length you need and lay the flashing down the center, pressing it into place in the valley, but avoid creasing. Secure it with roofing nails well up from the center.

Sometimes roll roofing is used for flashing. Roll roofing is in rolls rather than shingles and usually is of lighter weight than shingles. It is applied the same way as flashing. I am not sold on this method, but if I used it I would double the thickness. Cut the bottom layer at least 2" narrower than the top layer. Another method which does not use flashing is to overlap the shingles as the roof is laid. I will describe this process later. This method is better than the roll roofing, in my opinion, because the weight of material is heavier. I used aluminum flashing, then also used this method to provide double protection. Valleys are weak points in roofing.

The next step is to lay 15# building paper for underlayment. It comes in 36" rolls. Apply roofing tar along the edge of the roof to a width of 3-4". Do not make the coat too thick or it will melt in the sun and run down your eaves.

Roll the roofing along the edge and nail the paper into place with special nails. These are roofing nails with a head about an inch square (or use roofing nails along with plastic heads you purchase separately). Apply tar to the top 2" inches and apply the next layer. Side laps should be 6". Nail the felt into place and continue to the ridge. If you intend to install the ridgeline ventilation, follow the instructions that come with the material. Otherwise, lap the paper over the ridge about 6" onto the other side. Repeat the process on the opposite side of the roof, again overlapping the paper across the ridgeline as before.

Which side of the roof should you lay first? One principle of roofing is that everything should be installed with edges downwind. This means your overlaps should face away from the direction of prevailing winds. In much of the U.S., prevailing winds come from the northwest, so laps should point east and south. To accomplish this with roofing, you begin your application on the east or south side, allowing the north or west side to overlap the former.

Many roofers do not apply 15# roofing paper at all. They simply apply the shingles directly onto the decking. With the improved quality of roofing, the tar paper is less crucial than it used to be. The paper is an added protection against roof leaks. Use your own judgment whether to apply it, but you should know that all of the roofing guides I have consulted recommend the underlayment, and even urge the use of two layers if the pitch is less than 2 inches per foot. The better the roofing, the less the risk.

Laying the roofing

There are many kinds of roofing. The most common is the type that has three tabs, but it is not the best kind. Its weakness lies in the space between the tabs. Water seeks the lowest point, which is this space. Whereas the rest of the roofing has three layers when complete, the cutout area has two. A worn roof often looks fine from the ground, but when examined more closely is found to be badly worn between the tabs. Better designs include the T-lock, the French lap, and the diamond. The problem is that many building supply stores stock only the tab roofing. The choice of colors, availability, and appearance make it the choice of most homeowners and builders. Its widespread use also makes it cheaper. This was my choice in spite of its weakness simply because I did not want to track down the other types. If you want to take the extra time to locate them, the other types are better. The supplier probably will instruct you on how to lay them.

Your first layer of the tab roof is laid backwards, with the tabs up. It provides an underlayment for the next layer. If this is not done, the 15# underlayment will be exposed between the tab cutouts. Lay this layer along the outer edge of the drip edge. Some roofers overlay the first layer ½" (about the width of your finger) over the eave to keep the flow of rain farther from the facing.

Another rule of roofing: Never have a seam over a seam. To avoid this problem, your roofing must be staggered. You do this by cutting off portions of tabs. Each tab is 12" on center of the cutouts. Cut six inches off the rake edge of the tab, lap the longer piece over the eave edge about ¼", and nail it into place. The overlap keeps the water from pulling back under the roofing. Nail it above the cutouts high enough to be covered by the overlapping shingle but low enough so the nail will pass through the layer beneath. Also nail it the rake end. The adjacent full shingle is butted against the end and nailed, and the process continues along the roof.

You can continue along the eave all the way to the opposite end of the roof, or you can lay three or four shingles and start up with the next layer. Most roofers do the latter; it allows you to work in one place longer. It is easier to lay the first several layers from below if possible, from a ladder or scaffold. Otherwise, you have to bend over from upslope.

To begin the next layer, cut 12", a full tab, off the first shingle and nail the longer length into place. The next full shingle is butted against it and the process continued. The next layer begins with a cutoff of 18", a tab and a half. Cut an additional 6" off the first shingle of each succeeding layer, continuing through and including the last 6" piece of shingle. As you lay higher and higher layers, you will continually extend the roofing along the eave. After you complete the layer that begins with a 6" piece, you start the process over again with a full shingle. Save the waste from your cuts to use on the opposite rake.

You will notice that a layer of tar is already applied to the underside of each tab, covered with a thin piece of clear plastic. In the sun, the plastic will dissolve and the tar will adhere to the surface below it. This is to keep the wind from blowing the tabs up. In past years, tar spots had to be applied by the roofer, an aggravating job. If you happen to run across roofing that does not have the asphalt strips or dots applied, don't buy it; find another supplier.

The method just described is the most common. A variation is to cut your shingles every four inches instead of 6", producing a different visual effect.

The easiest way to lay roofing is to use the right tools. A special roofer's hammer is available. You can measure your roofing cuts with it, and it has a razor blade inset into it for cutting the material. Using regular tools is slower, but I chose to do so rather than invest in a tool I use so rarely. I used a linoleum knife (hook blade) to cut the material. A regular utility blade works fine, too. Hold a small square onto the cut to make sure it is straight and scribe the shingle on the back side. (If you try to cut from the top, the roof aggregate will quickly dull your knife.) A scribe mark is all that is necessary; the roofing breaks easily and cleanly. Cut dead center between the tabs. I use a regular hammmer with a smooth head for nailing.

You should strike a chalk line the length of the roof about every three layers in order to maintain a straight line. If you are a novice at laying roofs, strike a line for each of the first three layers; after that, you probably will have developed an eye for the task and a line every three layers will work fine. Measure from the eave up the rake on both ends of the roof. Determine how much exposure you want for the tabs, generally 4", and strike your lines accordingly. If you do not discipline yourself to do this, you will almost surely end up with an uneven roof, especially if you have help. Everyone will lay the roofing with different eyes for measuring.

It is quite possible that your roof structure is not absolutely perfect since you are building a house with more or less standard tools. One end of the ridgeline may be a bit higher than the other. If you have this problem, you can hide the discrepancies by creating a random pattern. Cut your shingles on a 5" pattern rather than 6" or 4". Do not use any piece less that 3" wide along a rake.

While we're on the subject of tools, consider clothing. Roofing is hard on clothes. The aggregate wears holes even in denim. The best solution is to wear something you don't mind ruining. Wear rubber-soled shoes. When working on a roof, do not step on loose shingles or anything else that is not nailed down. The aggregate is like tiny marbles that cause the loose material to slip, and it can happen in a flash. If you begin to fall, throw your body backward and spread your arms and legs. You may be bruised a bit, but not so badly as if you fall off the roof.

A roof with a 4" rise per foot is not too steep to work on with relative safety. The higher the rise, the more risk to the roofer. You can purchase or rent braces that support boards to give you a sort of scaffold on which to stand. The braces fasten to the roof in such a way as not to damage your shingles. Check with a building supplier for safety techniques for steep roofs.

A third rule of roofing is that laps always must be the upper over the lower. This point should be obvious, but novice roofers often forget it. As you plan your roofing process, think ahead to what situations you may run into. For example, a lower roof that ties into a higher roof should be laid first so the roofing of the higher slope can lap over that of the lower. To observe this rule, lay the barn roof last. The upper-over-lower rule applies also to every other circumstance, such as flues and chimneys. Never depend on roofing cement to overcome a violation of this rule.

Back to the roofing process. You have completed the roofing on both slopes of the roof, cutting the shingles at the ridgeline. To complete the job, you lay tabs onto the ridgeline itself, called ridgecaps. (If you add a ventilation ridge, it serves in place of the ridgecaps.) This is done by cutting shingles into thirds, one tab per piece. Begin laying the tabs at the end of the ridge that is away from the prevailing winds. Place a coat of roofing asphalt at the beginning edge and place a piece so that it overlaps both sides of the ridgeline equally. Set a nail on each side, placed so that they will be covered by the next piece. Lay the next piece over the preceding one so that the non-aggregate side is covered and secure it with nails. Continue this process the length of the ridge. The nails will be exposed on the last piece, but it will be above the overhang. Cover the nail heads with a bit of asphalt and you are done.

Valleys

If your design is like mine, or you otherwise have one roof tying into another one, the valleys created need special treatment. When two roofs of the same height and pitch join at the ridgeline, you can lay either roof first. When laying the first roof, you have a choice when you come to the valley, as mentioned earlier. You do not really need flashing for this type of structure unless you want extra insurance if you follow this procedure:

Continue your shingle run down into the valley and far enough up the other side so that about 8" of the opposite decking is covered. Leave a slight concave shape at the bottom to avoid creasing, which may break the shingles. When you lay the connecting roof, the shingle line will end dead center in the bottom of the valley (photo 11).

Remember our rule: all overlaps must be from above. If you continue the shingles of the overlapping roof beyond the valley midpoint, you will create an edge that faces up. That edge is vulnerable to the erosive force of rain and eventually will create problems. Strike a chalkline up the midpoint of the valley. As you come to the valley with each layer of shingles on the adjoining roof, cut it so that its edge falls onto the line. Apply a 4" border of asphalt along the underside of the overlap and press it into place.

Barn roof

Your biggest problem of laying the barn roof is to make sure the shingles come together in a straight line above where the adjoining roof's ridge meets the barn roof. To plan for this, place a long level against the barn roof, using a long board if necessary, on top of the ridge of the lower roof. Strike a line and continue it out each way to the rakes. Mark the line at three-foot increments (the width of a shingle) from rake to rake. Use the increments to plan how to place your tabs so the spacing will be even when you come above the intervening ridgeline. Next, mark 4" increments down each rake from the line. If the increments reveal a variation, make whatever adjustments are needed by exposing slightly more or less of each layer up to the line on both sides. Once above the roof union, the rest of the shingles are laid in normal fashion. The only other adjustment I had to make was at the elbow of the barn roof. The bend was too severe for the pre-applied asphalt to hold, so I nailed the tabs and covered the heads with asphalt.

By the time we finished the roofing, it was early December and very cold. We wore insulated coveralls, gloves, and wool caps, not a good way to end a project or a good time to lay roofing, which becomes brittle and hard to cut. But we had the structure under roof and protected for the winter, so we could rest for a while.

Chapter 6

Dry in the Structure

You Choose the Next Step

I do not like working in cold weather, so I let the project rest until spring. Through the winter months I fretted and thought about what to do next. I could begin laying the floor and installing the exterior siding, or I could complete the porch.

By the time warm weather returned, I had decided to complete the porch next, for two reasons. First, my adult Bible study class was anxious to see my progress; we planned a cookout. Second, I wanted a place under roof and floored, a level place to work and a place to rest out of the sun. The porch is 8' x 24', a fairly large area, and is a simple job.

Building the Porch

I purchased the porch materials because I wanted pressure-treated lumber. I used 2 x 8s to span the 8-foot space between beams and set them on 16" centers.

I set the ends of the joists 3/4" in from the edge of the porch sill in case I decided to add a facing board later. I ran the joists from that point to the centerpoint of the house sill beam. The joists for the interior flooring would abut these, giving a resting place of 2 3/4" for each joist on the 5 1/2" beam. The outer joists were fitted between the verticals and to run along the edge of the sill beams. I used 1 x 6 pressure-treated deck flooring, which is thicker than regular 1 x 6 lumber.

When you lay the deck boards, stagger the joints. If you use 8' lumber, for example, alternate every other run by starting it with a 4' board. The floor is both stronger and more attractive. If your lumber is new, you can jamb the boards tightly together; they will shrink to leave about the right crack between them. If the lumber is old, use a 16-penny nail to space them apart. Ask your lumber dealer if you are in doubt.

Avoid using smooth-shanked nails. They will work out and your decking will twist and warp. Use spiral decking nails or zinc-coated screws. Neither will rust; but screws are much easier to drive, if you use a drill motor, and can be removed without destroying the wood if repairs are needed.

Laying the Flooring and Blackboard

Due to the frequent rain in Tennessee, I did not want to lay my entire floor before applying the exterior siding. Our slanting rains from the northwest would soak four to six feet of flooring every time. I decided to work in 8' sections, applying both blackboard and flooring one section at a time. For clarity, though, I shall describe the processes separately. The enclosed walls also would protect my power equipment. Moreover, a variety of work is more pleasant than the tedium of one task at a time.

I made my floor joists from the log supply I had purchased. As stated earlier, I saved the rounded side cuts that had good lumber, stacking them carefully on edge and with good air circulation. I worked my way through the supply and laid aside those that were thick enough to provide a 2" board eight feet long. For the rest, I cut the joists as I needed them from logs. The sawmill work is loud, dirty, and tedious, so I cut enough joists for each 8' section of floor as I needed them rather than spend several days on the sawmill. Each section required 11 full-length joists and two more that run on top of the sill beams. These two each are cut into roughly 4' sections to fit between the vertical beams. By checking my stock carefully, I was able to make use of short logs and side cuts that otherwise might have become firewood. I set these shorter pieces one inch in from the outside edge of the sill beams to leave space for the siding. They are toenailed between the verticals. Where diagonal braces interfere, the joists are cut to fit the angle.

The flooring should extend to the outside of these joists, filling the space between the beams, so measure for your centers from that point. Draw a line down the center of the next beam beyond the one your porch joists rest on and mark it for 16" centers. Recheck the measurements from each porch joist to this line before you cut the joists, in case the sill beams have warped just a bit. Note each measurement and cut your joists to those sizes.

As you nail the joists into place, using 16-penny nails, apply cross braces for extra strength and to keep the floor from squeaking, as described for the second-story floor. I made mine from scrap lumber, of which I had plenty. Select two straight joists, unwarped and untwisted, and hold a piece of wood (about 1 1/2" square) diagonally across the ends, from the bottom of one joist to the top of the other. Mark the angles with a pencil and use it as a model to make a stockpile of braces. These are easily done on a chop saw, or you can set your table saw to make the cuts by using both the guidebar and the slider set to the proper angle. A circular saw will work in a pinch.

One line of braces down the midpoint of the joists should be sufficient. If any joist is twisted, hammer one or more additional braces into place to force it to correctness.

You are ready now for the flooring. Each 8-foot section requires six 4 x 8 sheets of plywood or pressboard. Standard flooring is 3/4", though some flooring is slightly less than that and meets standards. Be sure your supply is consistent. I purchased my plywood as I needed it and made the mistake of not checking the thickness each time. Even though I bought it from the same supplier each time, I wound up with slightly different dimensions. Unfortunately, I did not notice until later. When I laid floor tile, I had to use floorstone to smooth out the ridges.

When you are ready to put in your floor, you may want to lay plastic sheeting to cover the entire ground area under the house, as further protection against bugs as well as moisture. To be absolutely sure, you should pay for guaranteed termite treatment. Clear debris away from the area regularly; make sure wood is not in contact with the ground.

In typical frame construction, the floor is built after the foundation. It forms a platform onto which the walls are constructed. The process followed in a timber and beam house is to construct the frame first, then fill in the flooring. This is called ballooning. The method requires you to make cuts in the floor material to fit around the vertical beams. Because of these cutouts, it is not possible to use full 8' lengths in the corners. You must cut these sections into 4 x 4 squares. If the fitting had to be done around the verticals only, a 4 x 8 sheet perhaps could be notched and dropped into place with a little forcing. But the flooring also must be fitted around the diagonal braces.

Measuring all these details requires considerable patience. I found a tri-square to be useful. At the corners you will be working with two walls, so take it slow and be careful. "Measure twice and cut once," the saying goes. Make your cuts as precise as possible. If you leave gaps due to miscuts, fill them from below by making close-fitting cuts from scrap plywood of any thickness and attaching them with 1 1/8" screws. Now or later, fill the space with filler.

Use 1 1/2" flooring nails, with ridges down the shanks, not smooth-shank nails which will work loose.

Applying wall sheathing

Wall sheathing is the material that goes on before the siding. I used blackboard because it is cheaper than the aluminum type underlayments, but the R value is less. Blackboard is a pressed fiber material that produces an awful dust when cut. As with most sheathing, it comes in 4 x 8 sheets. Assuming your verticals are 8 feet, top to bottom a sheet should fit exactly into each section. It is a good idea to measure first, though. If you set your vertical beams on 4' centers, the width of the sheathing will be less and so must be trimmed on one side.

To apply the material, you must have a surface along each edge to nail it onto. The grooves cut into all but the corner verticals are ready to receive the sheathing. The floor joists are properly inset equal to the depth of the grooves. The diagonal braces were cut to 3 ½" to match the grooves, so they need no further work. Some beams, however, were not grooved: the upper and lower horizontals and the 8 x 8 corner verticals. These require that 2 x 4s be added. These can be rough lumber, just so their width is the same as the space allowed on your verticals, 3 1/2" in my case. I planned this dimension early on in case I ran out of materiel and had to purchase stock lumber.

Some of the 2 x 4s will have to be fitted with slanted cuts: the verticals that intersect the diagonal braces and the upper and lower horizontal 2 x 4s that abut the braces at the top and bottom. Actually, you can use 1 x 4s for the horizontals and also for the verticals that attach to the 8 x 8 corner beams.

Once these additional boards are in place, the sheathing may be applied. The easiest way to mark the blackboard is for one person to hold it in place and another to trace the cut mark from inside. If you work alone, hold it in place with a few screws, easily removed after you trace the line. Cut the material with a circular saw. A saber saw raises much less dust but is much too slow. Be sure to wear safety glasses; this material flies everywhere and makes a real mess. This unpleasantness may be reason enough to pay a bit extra and use the aluminum-backed material.

Nail the blackboard into place with sheetrock nails. I used the same type as for flooring. If you have not added the verticals that complete the rough opening of your windows, do so now. Photo 12 (back cover) shows the blackboard applied, with windows in; the windows were installed much later. To protect my floor from rain, before adding the windows I cut some of the rough plywood to size which I had used for the temporary second floor. I screwed the pieces into the window openings. I only did this on the windward side, leaving the leeward side and the porch area open for ventilation and light. Very little rain came in from those directions.

I had a sense of elation every time I completed an 8-foot section. The floor joists came first, then blackboard, then the plywood floor. Each time, I added to my work space and comfort. Looking back, it is clear I could have gained more floor space faster if I had sheathed in only the windward side as I laid the floor. Since little rain comes in on the east side, the plywood was pretty safe. I could have added the blackboard at my leisure on that side with a good bit of floor to work on.

Installing Windows and Doors

Depending on your design, you may install your windows before or after you apply the siding. You can make your own windows, of course, but I decided to purchase mine, primarily because I wanted double pane insulation. You will choose between brickmold, which comes already on, or frames without facings. For these, you make your own facings out of material compatible with your siding. The window frames will come with primer coat already applied to the weather-exposed parts. Stain cannot be applied over primer, so you will select a paint that is compatible with the treatment you apply to your siding.

You can stain the facings you make, of course. The rest will be painted. When I was ready to paint my windows, I stained a piece of poplar scrap and took it to the paint supplier to select a color that blended well. You can paint the windows as you install them or wait and do all of them at once, which is what I chose to do.

I ordered the first-story windows without moldings and made them myself out of poplar to match the siding. The result is excellent (photo 13). The construction is not difficult. Take measurements along each edge of the frame; these are applied to the inside edge of the molding. Cut 45-degree angles from the marks with a chop saw. (I had to turn each piece over and cut it a second time due to the capacity of my chop saw blade.) With the window frame laying flat, arrange the pieces and fasten them with finish nails along the inside edges. Drive finish nails through the corners to secure the joints and keep them flush; you probably will want to predrill the holes.

Follow the installation instructions that come with the windows. It is a simple procedure to plumb and level the frames and secure them. Particularly with your larger windows, only a small space will remain between the edge of the window and the next vertical beam. Your facings can cover this space. For your smaller windows, you can fill the space with the same siding used on the house, for uniformity (photo 14), but as an alternative you could use one vertical board.

For the second floor, I ordered the four windows with brick mold attached. This decision was simply to avoid the need for additional molding since my stock was low. The second-story siding (next chapter) fit flat against the wall, so I did not feel the different style would be noticed. As it turned out, the brick molding looks very good, but if I had not been low on poplar I would have made these facings (photo 1).

.It is most efficient to install the exterior doors at this time. I did not do so because of the schedule I was following. I wanted to make my own doors from some of the oak Greg and I harvested before we began the project, and I did not believe I could afford the time before cold weather set in. As an alternative, I used a couple of old screen doors and a couple of sidelights I had from sometime before. I installed the sidelights temporarily in one part of the section where the doors were to go. Then I hung the screen doors to fill the rest of the space; they overlapped the sidelights, but this was not a concern (seen in photo 12). I only wanted to keep the rain off my floor. I covered the screen doors with clear plastic. The system worked well and took the pressure off of me for making the doors and frames. However, I did install the sliding door that opens onto the porch since it is on the windward corner

Door frames are simple to make. You simply cut out a rabbet groove in each vertical to accept the horizontal at the top (diagram 25), which you secure with finishing nails, square the corners, and nail temporary angle braces to maintain 90-degrees while you install the frame. Allow 1/2" clearance on each side and top for plumbing the frame. Shim the assembly and nail it into the rough lumber. Screw the threshold into place and your frame is done. Actually, you will find it cheaper and much easier to buy the complete unit, but you may prefer to scrounge an old door somewhere to add personality to your project; or, like me, build the door yourself.

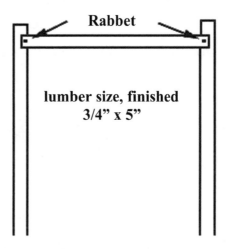

Diagram 25

Front doors typically are 36", back doors 32". These measurements are for the door itself; frames and clearances must be added to determine the rough opening. For a 36" door, allow 3/4" for each vertical of the frame, plus 1/2" for clearance on each side, giving a total width for the rough opening of 38 1/2". Use an existing beam for one side and add double 2 x 4s to form the other side. The 2 x 4s will be covered with siding. As with the windows, the small place remaining between the door frame and the beam can be filled easily with a 1 x 6 vertical board or smaller, or with small pieces of siding as described for the windows. If you use siding, the pieces are so small they tend to split when nailed. To avoid this, drill guide holes.

If you choose to make your own door, here are a couple of ways to do the job. The simplest way is to cut several lengths of 1" lumber to 80" and lay the

97

pieces side by side to make a 36" width. Then cut enough 1" lumber to 36" lengths to run crossways over the longer pieces. For an outside door, place plastic sheeting between the layers, or--better--tongue and groove your outside pieces. Place the assembly onto a flat surface. Begin by laying a 36" piece at one end and screwing it onto the first long piece, using at least four 1 1/4" screws (or short enough not to go through). Make sure it is exactly 90 degrees to the long pieces. Select decorative screws; they will show.

Set a clamp close to the crosspiece and pull the boards snugly together. If you have a helper, have him or her stand on another crosspiece laid across the boards to keep them from buckling from the pressure of the clamp. Tighten the clamps and run the screws through the rest of the pieces. Leave the clamp in place until you set another one a little farther along the boards. Leapfrog the clamps until all the crosspieces are screwed into place, 4 screws through each crosspiece into each long piece. This style door is quite strong, and heavy.

The old-fashioned Z-braced door is another option. For this style, use tongue and groove wood and both glue and screw the Z-braces into place.

15

Another method of door construction is to cover a pressboard core with hardwood. This is the method I decided on (photo 15). The frame consists of solid oak--two verticals, kickboard, header, and center horizontal--which I connected with deep mortises and tenons. Two pieces of 3/4" pressboard are set into grooves cut into the inside edges of the oak frame. Thin oak slats, overlapped 1/2" with a simple L cut, were glued onto the pressboard.

The sliding door is not difficult to install if you plan the rough opening for

98

it. Follow the instructions that come with the assembly. You have a choice of swinging doors (French) or sliding, and a wide choice of materials. Prices range up to two thousand dollars or more for hardwood French doors with cut glass insets. I got mine second-hand (photo 7).

After you install the sliding or French door, you will have some trim work left to do to completely eliminate all openings around the door. You can cut your trim from your wood stock to fit the need and your taste. Stuff insulation into all openings and run trim around the edges of the door, overlapping onto the metal. You probably have a small open space between the header and the upper beam. Stuff insulation into this space and cover it with a wood plate or trim. Be sure to sure to caulk every possible crack.

Chapter 7
Making and Applying
Exterior Siding

You can make or purchase your exterior siding. If you purchase it, your choices are many. As it turned out, I ran short of materials and had to adjust. My first story was completed with material I cut from my log supply. I still had a fair supply of rounded side cuts from my logs and several logs remained as well. I used almost all my remaining stock for siding, but it took all I had. I finished the gable ends of the barn style second story and the gable above the porch with exterior plywood siding.

Siding options

You have several options for the type siding you make from you own stock.

Option 1: Vertical board and batten. This style has boards running vertically. First you nail boards one against another along the wall. The joints then are covered with 2" - 3" strips (battens). This option is easy to make and install, but it requires at least one horizontal cross brace halfway between the sill and the header. Additional support above and below windows is not needed.

Sawmill your lumber to 3/4" if you want to apply it rough, at least 7/8" if you want to plane it. To determine the width to cut your boards, measure the distance between vertical beams and determine what width will work best in multiples. You can use one standard width all around the house if your vertical beams are equidistant. If they are not, you need to center full-width boards and place a narrower board of equal width on each side.

This method is simple and quick, but in my opinion the style is not compatible with a timber and beam construction. The vertical style diminishes the prominence of the vertical beams.

Option 2: Drop siding. There are a variety of types of drop siding. Each piece fits over the lower one by some sort of cut, such as the rabbet, tongue and groove, or shiplap, the last being most common. If you want one of these types, visit your building supply store and look at their stock. With a little imagination and planning, you can figure out ways to make some of these cuts on a table saw. Others will require routing.

Option 3: Bevel and bungalow. The only difference between these two styles is thickness and width. In each case, lumber is ripped on an angle to result in a thicker lower edge and a thinner upper edge. The boards are overlapped. This style can be made with the saw mill I was using. It is the style I used and the one I will describe (photo 1, 21, 22).

Make the siding

First, determine how much exposure you want for you siding. A standard is 4 inches, but more is ok. Each board should overlap the one below it by 2 inches, so you need 6" stock for a 4" exposure. You might want to draw a wall to scale on paper, including all features, and draw lines to represent 4", 5", and 6" exposures. This will help you get a visual feel for what each exposure will look like.

When you determine the dimensions of your siding, use the mill to square logs to accommodate your decision. Set the mill to cut planks 1 1/8" thick if you intend to plane them, 1" for rough-cut application. The extra thickness is because you will get two pieces of siding from each plank.

Your planks from rounded sidecuts are treated the same way, but you can cut them to width on a table saw. If you cut them to length for ease of handling, cut them a couple of inches longer than you need, or multiples of lengths. Mark a straight line down one side of the plank and cut it either on a table saw or circular saw. If you are careful, the cut will be straight enough for the next step.

To rip the opposite side, set the table saw 1/8" over the width you want, say 6 1/8", and rip the planks. Reset the saw to 6" and resaw the first side to even it up. This process will give you good lumber.

Once you have a sufficient stock of 1 1/8" planks cut to the proper width, run both sides through the planer. Plane them evenly by running all of your stock through before you change the setting. When the planks are smoothed to your liking, you are ready to cut them to siding.

Set up a jig on which to cut the siding. I built a taller-than-usual sawhorse four feet long and high enough so I would not have to bend over to work the sawmill. I screwed a piece of wood on one end of the sawhorse about half the thickness of the plank; this served as a stop to keep the plank from moving forward. Your first cut may take part of this brace, but that is no problem. A bigger problem is that the sawblade, as it begins its cut, throws the plank violently to the side. To solve this, run a screw on the side of the sawhorse at the end opposite the stop. Sink it to about half the thickness of the plank; be sure the head is low enough not to catch the sawblade. Place the plank against this screw.

Lay *two* planks onto the "sawhorse" jig, the bottom one firmly pressed against the braces described above. You will cut the *bottom* one. The top one is necessary for spacing, as the sawmill cannot be set for a thinner bias cut.

Set the sawmill blade at an angle. You will have to practice to get this right. Set the sawmill so the plate is as close to the motor as possible. The closer it is, the more the weight is supported by the plank rather than by your arms. When you have it placed where you want it, set the guide finger as far in as it will go. Now you are ready to set the blade at an angle.

If you have a helper, he can support the mill while you set the adjustment, or you may devise a system to support the mill at exactly the position you want. Otherwise, you must take the sawmill off your work in order to set it. With the mill setting on the plank, estimate how much you need to raise or lower each end to get the correct angle for your slice. Ideally, from a 1" thick plank, about 1/8" should be left for the thinner side and 7/8" minus the kerf for the thicker side, but these measurements are not critical. You probably will have to lift the saw back and forth several times before you have the setting like it should be.

Once the setting is made, begin your cuts. The only really tricky part is starting. Begin at a severe angle at the left corner of the plank. Once the cut is started, you should have no more trouble. Continue the cut just as you would normally. When you apply the siding, the rough sides will be inside, the smooth sides out.

Cut at least enough stock to complete one 8-foot section (two 4-foot vertical sections). If your walls are 8', you will need 24 pieces of siding per 4-foot section, assuming a 4" exposure. The jig setup takes a bit of time, so make the most of each session.

After you have cut your stock, go through it and discard the bad pieces. A few boards may have deteriorated; others may have knots that fall out during the cutting. You want no flaw that will allow rain to seep through.

Install the siding

The next step is to mark on the vertical beams where each piece of siding will go. This marking will save considerable work time. First, place a level on the sill beam. If it is off level, measure six inches above the <u>highest</u> end, then with your level make a corresponding mark on the other end. Make your marks in the groove so the siding will cover them. Going up, make a mark every four inches from this first mark to the top of the verticals.

Before you cut the siding to specific lengths, check the measurements between each of the opposing marks and make notes of the lengths. In spite of my efforts at accuracy, the distance between the vertical beams was not constant. Slight warping occurred over the several months the framing was exposed to the weather. You probably will have run into this problem already, if there is one, when you applied the blackboard. At any rate, measuring takes little time and may will save extra effort and aggravation later.

Square one end of each piece of siding. Then follow your notes for measurements. Keep the pieces in order. You will want the bottom pieces first, so either make your cuts from top to bottom of your list, or turn the stack over to apply the siding. If your space is 8' high, you will notice that the top piece will be 4" rather than 6". Rip 2" off this piece, but keep both pieces.

Use #8 zinc-coated finish nails to apply the siding, one nail to each side. The nails will be exposed, so a non-rust type is essential. Set the nail just above the top of the piece below. Start at the bottom by nailing the 2" strip left from the top piece of siding. This piece provides the underlap for the first full-width piece. Set it flush onto the sill beam, whether or not the beam is absolutely level. Nail it with one nail at each end. Align the top of the next full piece on a level with the marks you previously made and nail it into place. Continue adding the siding, the tops aligned with the 4" marks; this will give 2" of overlap.

When you finish with the 8' section, you may apply sealer or wait. You do not want the siding to darken from weathering, so if you are working slowly, I recommend you apply sealer. I decided to add the stain when I completed an entire side, which took two or three weeks during which it rained a couple of times. The wood did not darken in that length of time.

The pictures in this book show the house stained. I much prefer this look. Unfortunately, the walls mildewed and showed ultraviolet damage after two years. I had to clean the walls, then I decided to use paint. I picked a color close to the color of the stain (photo 22). While paint does not allow grain to show, it lasts a lot longer. Which to use is your call.

Caulk before you stain or paint. Select a caulk as close to the color of the stain as possible. Wisdom calls for a high quality caulk. This construction method requires a lot of caulking. I did not record how many tubes, but it was a bunch. You should not scrimp on this step. It will save in both deterioration of materials and in fuel bills. Caulk everywhere weather might enter the structure: around window frames and along the top, bottom, and sides of vertical beams. Also caulk any fault in the wood, such as cracks in knotholes.

As with the beams, I applied three coats of stain preservative on the siding and the window facings. I also restained the exposed parts of the beams. The caulking absorbed enough of the stain to cause it to blend very well. Remember there is a window of time when caulk will accept paint or stain.

105

Continue the process all around the house.

The second-story siding

As noted earlier, I had to use a different siding on the second story since I was running low on poplar. After considering various options, I finally decided to use 4 x 8 exterior plywood. The surface is roughcut, in contrast to the smooth siding on the first floor. This was my primary reluctance to use this material, but I finally decided the problem was minor. If you have enough material to continue the same application, you may want to consider other options anyway. The issue is altogether visual, apart from cost.

Whatever your siding choice, your cuts are going to be more complicated. If your design is a barn style roof as mine is, you have several angles to figure.

To work on the second floor section, you should have an extension ladder of at least 20 feet, preferably 24. Tape several layers of cloth around the ends that will rest against the siding; this will both protect the siding and keep the ladder more secure.

Check the level of your second story beam before you make any cuts. Your siding will be applied on each side of the center vertical beam that supports the ridgepole, so measure out each way from that midpoint. If the beam is off a bit, use a long level to mark your line as near the beam as possible. Then measure from the beam to the line at its highest point above the beam. This is the adjustment you will make in your first siding cut (diagram 26). I did one side of the vertical beam at a time, but the sequence does not matter. Check the plumb of the vertical beam; if it is off a bit, make the same type of adjustment.

If you are using lap siding, follow the same process for this section as you did for the first floor.

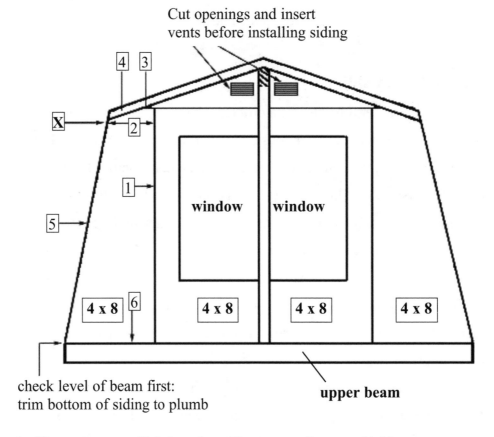

Cut openings and insert
vents before installing siding

window   window

4 x 8   4 x 8   4 x 8   4 x 8

check level of beam first:
trim bottom of siding to plumb

upper beam

1. If measurement #1 is less than 8", measure from vertical beam to cave angle

2. Measure level line from edge of siding to angle

3. If rise from beam is more than 8", measure level line from edge of siding to angle

4. Measure from angle at #3 to elbow

5. Measure from bottom angle to elbow

6. Measure at bottom from corner to angle

7. Transfer Measurements to 4' x 8' siding

8. Measurements #2, 3, 4 and 5 should meet at **X**

Diagram 26

My design includes a window in the area where the first sheet of siding was applied. Mark the cutout of the window by taking measurements up from the horizontal beam and out from the vertical beam. Alternatively, you can attach the plywood siding into place temporarily with long screws and mark the cutout from inside the window opening. This process is more accurate and probably faster, but it requires lifting the siding into place twice. If you do this, screw a piece of 2 x 4 into the horizontal beam flush with its top to support the weight of the plywood; this provides a footing on which the siding can rest. Afterward, fill the screw holes; the slight defacement won't show.

The next sheet of 4 x 8 siding will intersect the angles of the roofline. Depending on whether you have a triangular gable end or where your elbow of the barn style roof is placed, you may have to contend with either one or two angles. The cut is not all that difficult either way. See diagram 26. Before you figure the angle cut, adjust the bottom of the siding for any off-level that may exist.

The top space above the two panels is comparatively small. Measure this area using the same methods. Before you install the siding, however, install vents into the piece if you are working with plywood paneling. If you are applying lap siding, you will have to build a frame for the vent. Several types of vents are available from your building supply store. Check them out to determine which type you want to install and arrange your hole accordingly. I selected an inexpensive flat vent. This enabled me to cut out a hole a bit smaller than the vent and screw the vent directly onto the siding.

The area to be vented is between the ceiling and the roof, so the vent must be placed accordingly. Since eave vents are not possible on the side of the house with the intersecting roof, these gable vents are necessary for air flow. The upstairs ceiling has to be planned to allow space for passage of air from gable end to gable end.

At this point, the exterior of the house is complete. What a feeling! You can take your time doing the interior, enjoying the shelter as you choose. And you can work rain or shine.

Chapter 8

Finishing the Interior

Several steps are required to complete the interior: install the stairway if two-story, install the plumbing and fixtures, install the electrical wiring and fixtures, apply the interior walls, install the kitchen cabinets and any remaining constructions, and apply the trim and finish coats.

To provide light on dark days, I purchased three 4-foot fluorescent shop lights, two for downstairs and one for up, and tied them into the temporary wiring. I hung them from the overhead beams by running screws through the hanging chains that came with the fixtures.

The Stairway

The construction of a stairway turned out to be difficult because the length of run available was from the center beam to the outside wall, about 11'4". Since the distance is not long enough for adequate tread widths, a turn was required. The height of my ceiling from the floor is 8 feet, less 7 1/2" for the overhead beam. This became a factor I had not anticipated. The stairway runs parallel to the crossbeams, but when I figured the turn, I realized the crossbeam did not allow for enough head room.

I could have made the steps steep and shallow, as are often found in log cabins; but code should be followed carefully for your stairway, even if the structure will not be examined by a codes investigator. The safety of your family and guests is paramount. **Carpentry**, by Gaspar J. Lewis (New York: Sterling Publishing Co., Inc., 1984) contains a good description of options and methods of construction that I found quite helpful. After several fits and starts and modifying the processes to fit my timber and beam construction, here is the process I followed.

First, I decided that the minimum width of the stair should be 36 inches. This required me to move one of my upper floor joists, a fairly simple task. That done, I had a rectangular opening. I dropped a plumb line from each corner and marked the location precisely on the lower floor. When I connected the marks, my opening was exactly duplicated on the lower floor. One end of the rectangle abutted the outer wall.

To determine how many steps you need, assume that each riser will be 8". Measure the height from the lower floor to the upper floor and divide it by 8 inches. This gives you the number of risers you need. The result will not likely be exact, so use the next highest number. You will have one more riser than tread, not counting either floor as a tread.

My earlier planning was to install a landing two steps up from the lower floor, but my overhead beam remained a problem because the landing ate up a space of 3' x 3'. My final solution was to install angle steps, plus one more step at the bottom. The result is quite satisfactory (photo 16).

Mark the tread widths lightly onto the rectangle; these marks probably

will require adjusting. The relation-
ship between riser height and tread
width is exact. Gaspar points out
that the sum of one *riser* and one
tread should equal between 17 and
18 inches for safety (p. 275). *Codes
require that all risers must be the*

same height.. This is a safety requirement; people walking up a staircase will as-
sume they will lift their feet the same amount with each step. The depth of your
treads probably should be not less than 9 inches. You will have a one-inch overlap for each tread, giving at least a 10" footfall.

After I worked with the marks on the floor for a while, I needed one more
step than I had space for. To solve the problem, I decided to make the highest
tread the top surface of the upper beam. The end of a floor joist coming from the
other direction rested on this beam, so I had to cut it back. This left it dangling, a
minor problem solved by screwing a 2 x 10 brace onto the beam, then nailing the
joist end onto the brace.

I included three angle steps to make the turn at the bottom. If you follow
this process, be sure the narrow end of each step is wide enough to be safe. Diagram 27 shows the construction of the treads, newel, and stringers. The angled
lines represent the treads; the straight and dotted lines indicate the stringers. The
small ends of the treads are mortised into the newel. The wider ends of the angled steps form longer faces than the stringers can accommodate. These need to
be built out to pattern (described later). Be careful to make outside surfaces flush
so as the accept sheetrock or other wall treatment.

Once I was satisfied with the layout drawn on the floor, I was ready to install the stringers. I used three. Two run the full length from the upper beam to

112

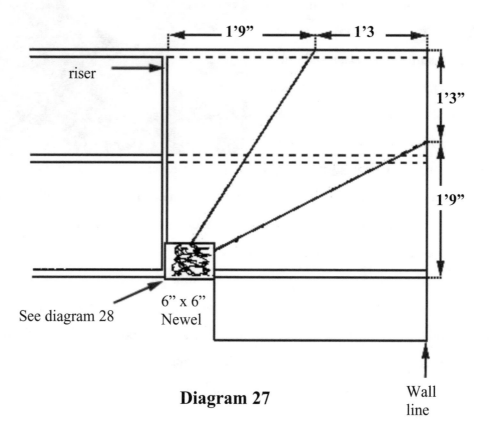

Diagram 27

riser

1'9"　　1'3

1'3"

1'9"

See diagram 28

6" x 6"
Newel

Wall
line

abut the wall at the bottom. The third stringer is anchored into a 5-inch thick newel post, which I cut from oak (photo 16). To receive the stringer, I used a combination of circular saw and chisels to cut a mortise 1" in from the edge and made it 1" deep.

To install the newel, I first determined its location, then nailed 1" x 2" oak pieces around its bottom, joined at the corners with 45 degree cuts. Once the stringer was attached the newel was pretty secure, and after the steps were attached it was very secure.

To install the stringers, you must determine what angle is required to butt against the upper beam and the wall at the lower end. I am not good at geometry and found this process to require considerable trial and error. I cut each end a bit at a time, conservatively, until I got it right. The second stringer is identical to the first. The third stringer that fits into the newel matches the others on its upper end. The angle on its lower end is the same as the other two, but obviously the board is shorter. When you measure for length, remember to add one inch to insert into the opening in the newel. Cut the corner off the lower end of this stringer so it will fit into the mortise on a level with the floor.

Once I had the angles on the first stringer cut, I set the stringer loosely in place. As yet, I had made no tread cuts. This is the next step. Use a level to mark a line to represent the tread. Following the line, use a carpenter's square to mark the other treads. Mark your riser height exactly square to your guide mark for the tread. You will find that you have no room for adjustment. The riser height will determine the tread depth. With the square against the riser mark and its heel at the top of the mark, draw a line for the next tread. Repeat the process for all risers and treads, using the exact measurements on the square each time.

Cut out for the treads by starting with a circular saw and finishing with a reciprocal or saber saw. Use the finished stringer as a model for the other two stringers.

When you set the stringers into place, check the level of the stringers each way and adjust as necessary. Very little adjustment, if any, should be required, but place shims at one end of the stringer or the other if necessary, preferably at the bottom. Use very hard wood or metal for shims; soft wood will compact over time. Fasten the stringers into place with 3" all-purpose screws.

The next step is to extend the stringer cutouts on which the angled treads will rest. This framing is best done with 3/4" plywood rather than 2 x, since the cutouts on which the treads will rest can be shaped as needed; the plywood can be cut as wide or deep as necessary. Begin with the outside long stringer. Find a mark on the wall that is level with the top angle tread and secure the plywood to the inside surface of the stringer. The plywood should be about 16" or so top to bottom. Mark on the plywood the line the top angle tread will follow (1' 9" in diagram 27). At that point, make a right-angle cut down for 8" (for the riser), then another right angle to that cut to go all the way to the wall. This will form the tread surface for the next tread down. Since the plywood is fastened to the inside of the stringer, a space is left on the outside which must be filled in before sheetrock can be added. Do this now or later.

Treads are attached in two steps, rough and finished. The rough treads do not overlap the risers, and they are mortised into the newel (diagram 28). Again, if your geometry is as poor as mine, this process will require some trial and error. Begin with the top angle tread. In my case, this was the third one up, fourth counting the extra step at the bottom. A support for the front edge of the tread must be added. Fasten a 2 x 4 to support the outside edge of the tread; attach one end to the inside of the stringers and toe-nail the other

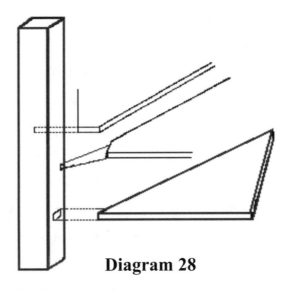

Diagram 28

end into the newel. Since the angle treads are wide and deep, an additional brace should be added in the center of each. Run it from the center of the 2 x 4 just described back to near the right-angle corner. Add a similar center brace to each step.

The top angle step, if it is like mine, has one right angle. The small end also has a right angle that runs only 2 1/2" to 3" (to be mortised into the newel). A line runs from the small end to connect with the longer side, forming two more angles. You may estimate the angle using an angle tool and straightedge, but you should cut a cardboard or light plywood model first so you can adjust as necessary. Be sure to add 1" for the mortise into the newel. Cut this mortise to the thickness of the rough tread before you attach the support (see mortise discussion below).

Use 3/4" plywood, not pressboard, for the rough treads, a lesson I learned by having a pressboard tread break on me. I caught myself but skinned a knee.

The next step down is a confusion of angles. A portion of the center stringer supporting the previous tread must be cut back. Nail a 2 x 4 between studs in the outer wall for this tread to rest on. Use plywood to extend the center tread to the wall, cutting down to the next tread level at the intersecting line (the line from the 1' 3" mark on the wall back to the newel). For the next step down, the lowest angle step, a support is run from this lower corner back to the newel. A 2 x 4 is set between the studs on a level for this lower step and a riser is set onto the floor and attached at the newel and wall.

Before you attach any supports that will be in the way, cut out the mortises in the newel. Establish the marks on the newel by using a 4' level from the wall support or other fixed point to the outside edge of the newel. Use a tri-square to transfer this mark to the inside edge of the newel. Notice in diagram 26 that the center angle tread is inset into the newel on both sides of the corner. Mark this line along the newel surface; this is the top of the mortise cut. When the mortises are completed, attach supports to the newel at the bottom of the mortises, the other ends to the wall braces. You are ready now to prepare a pattern and, when right, install the tread.

The treads above the angled ones are simple. Each one is a rectangle, except that the next one up from the angled ones has a cut in one corner to accommodate the newel post. Also, if you use the upper beam for a tread, that tread may need to be reduced in width.

Plumbing and fixtures

Installing plumbing is not beyond the skill of anyone who tackles a project as large as building a house. The details, however, are beyond the scope of this book. You should purchase one or two how-to books on plumbing, with lots of diagrams.

Plumbing breaks down into two areas: supply and waste. If you are using this book, you likely are not accessible to a sewer line and so must install a septic system. This is the only part of construction that I did not do myself even though the principles involved are fairly simple. A great deal of digging and heavy lifting is involved.

Contact the water department in the county or town where you are constructing your house. An agent will come to your property and run "perk" tests. A perk test indicates how well water absorbs (percolates) into the soil. The test may be as simple as digging a one-cubit hole, filling it with water, and timing how long it takes for the water to absorb into the soil. In places such as Tennessee, which has a great deal of limestone, perk tests are essential. A wrongly-placed septic system will result in contaminated water coming to the surface.

You will indicate to the agent where you want the septic tank located, so determine how you want your house to be placed on the lot before you call him. He will run his tests and otherwise examine your property, then prepare a diagram for placement of the septic tank and field lines. In my case, the septic tank was located a few feet from the house but the field lines were placed a considerable distance from the tank, due to limestone near the surface in the wrong places.

The theory of a septic system is that waste from the house goes into a tank where bacteria act on the waste. The size of the tank is part of the specifications drawn by the agent and is based on the size and number of bedrooms of the house it serves. The pipe that enters the septic tank is lower than the exit pipe. The tank fills with water to a certain point. Waste floats on top of the water and is acted on by the bacteria. When the water reaches the level of the exit pipe, it flows out to the field lines. The field lines have drain holes all along them and are set in gravel. The water runs through the drain holes and seeps through the gravel. By the time it completes the process, the water is safe.

You may want to do your own work of installing the drains from the house to or near the septic tank. The slope of this drain line is important. It must be sloped so the waste neither runs too fast nor moves too slowly; both can create clogging problems. A slope of 1/4" per running foot is proper. A plumbing book will advise on how to plan this system and tie in the various lines that exit the house.

The plumbing company I hired to install my septic system had to use an air hammer to break through limestone to set the tank. The installers left a short length of pipe extending out from the entrance side of the septic tank and capped it. When I completed my plumbing, all I had to do was remove the cap and attach the line from the house.

As you plan the placement of your fixtures, consider the points at which the fixtures will be attached to the plumbing. The pipe coming from an upstairs commode should run between floor joists of upper stories, if feasible; otherwise you will have to cut a large hole or holes in joists and then reinforce the joists. In my house, I had to do the second because of the direction I decided to run my joists. The task of cutting the holes and reinforcing the joists was not a daunting one, but it ought to be avoided if reasonable to do so.

The placement of a commode above a commode, or at least in close proximity to it, will aid greatly in the amount of materials and complication of your plumbing job. The same is true of sink, tub, and shower drains. If drains can use the same pipes, your work will be greatly simplified. Of course, the ultimate test of a well-planned house is how comfortable it is, so you will balance off the ease of plumbing with what you want in a house.

For the fairly small house I built, I decided to put most of my plumbing on the south wall. To cut large holes for plumbing pipes through my beams would have affected the integrity of the structure, so I built a dummy wall of 2 x 4s all along the inside of this one wall. The dummy wall carries no weight, so the size of the holes do not matter. All of the waste system except that for the washing machine runs through this dummy wall; the washing machine waste line runs under the floor and connects to the exit drain in the crawl space.

The first step obviously is to plan your fixtures. With the above comments in mind, draw a floor plan. A good plumbing how-to book will provide dimensions and clearances for fixtures. When you are satisfied with your floor plan, draw a wall elevation showing the plumbing, such as diagrams 29 and 30. Its preparation will call to mind factors you otherwise will not think of, and it is an invaluable aid in developing a materials list. I recommend buying extra pieces of everything. You'll save a lot of time in the long run and you can return materials you don't use.

The water source is the other area to plan. If you have a well, or plan to

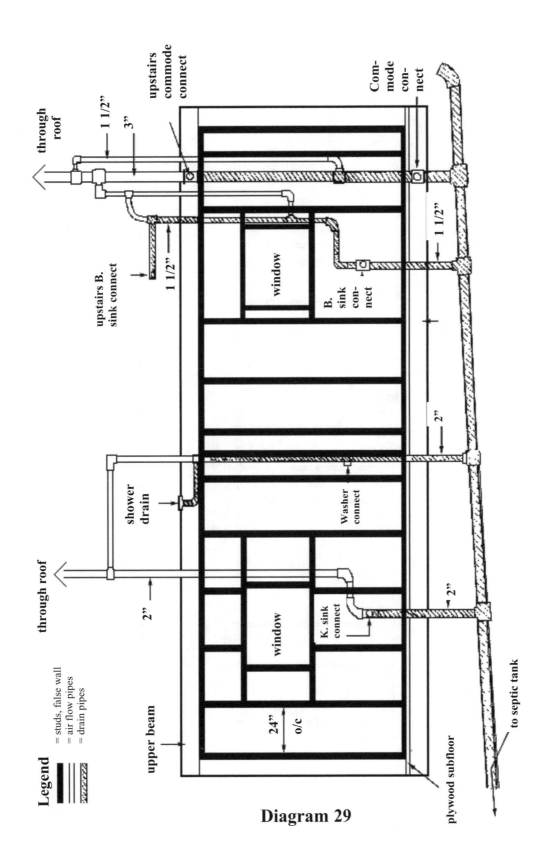

Diagram 29

120

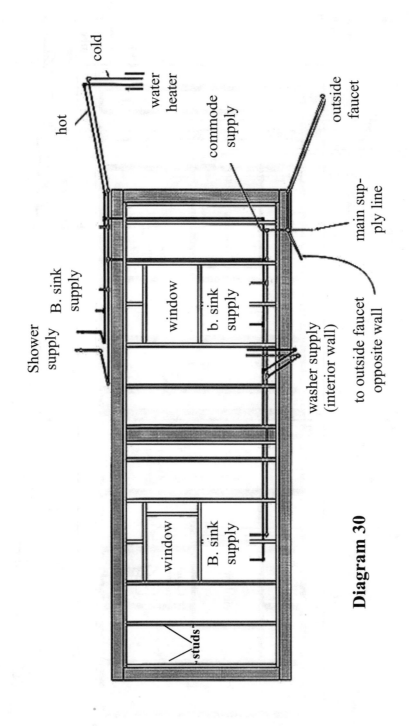

cold

hot

water
heater

commode
supply

outside
faucet

Shower
supply

B. sink
supply

window

b. sink
supply

main sup-
ply line

washer supply
(interior wall)

to outside faucet
opposite wall

window

B. sink
supply

studs

Diagram 30

dig one, or if you have a nearby stream with safe water, you will need to gather information about well types, pumps, pump houses, and tanks. If you have access to water lines, as I did, your work will be simpler.

I knew that city water would come to our area within a reasonable time, having kept in touch with neighbors. The cost of hooking up to the line when it came was about $1600. I figured that was considerably less than digging a well and installing the equipment. Even though I have a monthly water bill, I am drinking and using treated water.

I rented a ditch-digging machine to dig the water line from the road to the house, some 450 feet. Greg and I plotted our course. To determine the best route, mainly to avoid the limestone as much as possible, we ran a sharpened 1/2" steel rod into the ground to a depth of about 18 inches all along our planned line. We adjusted for the best route. When we began to dig, we ran into the occasional tree root, which we dispatched with hatchets. There was no way around all the limestone, which was much more difficult. The ditcher worked very well on dirt, not at all on the rock. We dug all we could with the ditcher, then returned the ditcher and rented an air hammer.

I learned from talking with the rental company that an electric air hammer is not powerful enough to break up limestone. An air hammer is required, and we took two kinds of bits. My body gave out pretty fast with this tool. Fortunately, Greg's youth stood us in good stead and he was able to do the bulk of the work, but he paid the price with very sore muscles. As he broke up the rock, I dug it out with a variety of probes and shovels.

One section of about fifty feet was so hard that Greg could not break it up even with the air hammer. We managed to dig and hammer down to about 12 inches. The freeze line in our area is 18 inches. I purchased high-quality foam insulation tubes and pushed them onto the water line. Since the insulation is designed for above-ground use, I assumed it would insulate well below ground. So far, after several winters, we have had no trouble with freezing.

We installed PVC pipe from the meter at the road all the way to the house, about 450', bringing it up out of the ground at the point where I wanted the line to enter the house. We capped it off and insulated it well. Later, after my house installation was complete, I would saw off the cap and connect the water lines.

Electrical wiring and fixtures

The installation of electrical wiring is much more difficult than plumbing. I had wired a room addition, a garage, and various smaller projects, but the wiring of an entire house required a great deal of study. I read and absorbed three how-to books, obtained a booklet on Marshall County codes from the Duck River Co-op and studied it carefully, and talked with a knowledgeable supplier and with the codes inspector.

Codes require electrical boxes to be placed at certain heights above floors and cabinet tops, and at certain distances apart. The supply conduit must be installed to specifications, the breaker box must be installed properly, breakers must match up with the breaker box manufacturer, loads must match, wiring must be run and used properly, and of course connections must follow specifications.

If your budget will allow, you will save yourself a lot of time and work by hiring an electrical contractor. If you decide to install the wiring yourself, be sure to prepare yourself well for the task. You don't have to learn electrical engineering, but you do have to understand the basics of how electrical current moves through the system, through fixtures in various combinations of hookups, and back to the breaker box. Do the job right. The money you save is ill-spent if

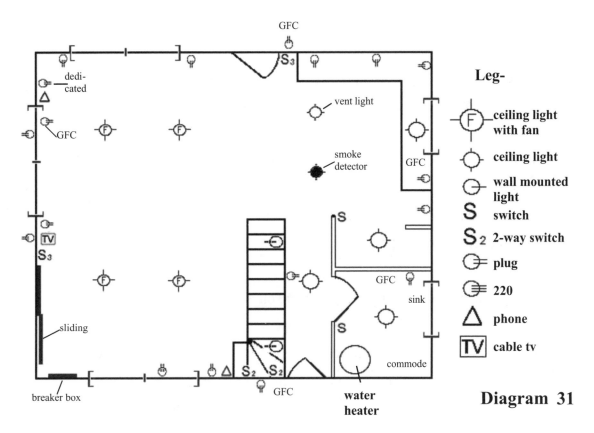

Diagram 31

Leg-

(F)	**ceiling light with fan**
-○-	**ceiling light**
◖	**wall mounted light**
S	**switch**
S₂	**2-way switch**
⊖	**plug**
⊜	**220**
△	**phone**
TV	**cable tv**

you lose your house to a fire.

Purchase a good how-to book on electrical projects and learn enough to plan the placement of your outlets and fixtures. Then purchase at least one more book and study it carefully. Prepare a diagram of outlets and fixtures to submit to the inspector before you start your work (diagram 31). Hopefully, the inspector will catch any major mistakes before you run the wiring.

On the diagram, indicate every plug you want and the placement of every fixture inside and outside. The how-to books will tell you symbols to use for different types of plugs and fixtures. Once you have all of this on paper, plan the circuit runs, following the load limits indicated in your how-to books. Buy a packet of colored pencils and use a different color for each circuit. When you are satisfied with the diagram, make color copies at an office supply house and take one to the inspector. He likely will have several suggestions even though you follow all the rules carefully as best you can.

When I received the inspector's tentative support, I began running the wiring. This task is compounded by the timber and beam construction. Holes have to be drilled through much thicker wood, and less working space is available. Before I began the runs, I sat down

124

thicker wood, and less working space is available. Before I began my runs, I sat down once more with my diagram and wrote out exactly what kind of wire to run for each part of each circuit: wall switch to plug, plug to fixture, etc. (such as 14-gauge wire, 2-wires plus ground, for a particular run, then switch to 3-wires plus ground for another part of the circuit). I plotted each circuit this way. The process uncovered some weaknesses in my plans. Sometimes I came up with a better way to combine plugs or fixtures in circuits; sometimes I came up with a better route for the wiring.

In addition to this planning, I wrote on a strip of tape what each circuit included, in sequence, and attached the tape to the wire at the breaker box. I also tagged the wires the circuit number on the breaker box. This tagging avoided considerable confusion later. With 17 circuits, a lot can be forgotten.

How-to books have diagrams to direct you on how to hook up all kinds of combinations. Once you get the hang of it, the instructions are simple to follow.

Generally, inspection is done after you have roughed in all the wiring and made the initial connections. All wiring must be left exposed, not covered with insulation or otherwise obscured. One thing inspectors are sensitive to is whether someone is trying to hide something. Your attitude should be that if something is done wrong, you want to know about it for your own safety and that of your family, friends, and guests. Cabinets have to be in place (at least in my area) so the inspector can be sure the plugs are the correct height above the surface.

After the rough-in inspection is approved, you will have to do the finish work connected with the outlets and fixtures. The sheetrock or other interior finish is applied, fixtures are installed, covers are put on the outlets, etc. Then the inspector returns for the final look. If he approves the installation, the electrical supply wires are attached to the house and the supply is turned on.

Wall treatment

Perhaps the simplest and most versatile wall treatment is sheetrock, and this is what I chose (photo 17). Just as with the blackboard on the outside, each 4 x 8 sheetrock has to be fitted into the timber frame. Applying the material is straightforward except for the cathedral ceiling. For this, we rented an apparatus that has arms to hold the sheetrock and a crank to raise it into place. We also laid heavy planks onto the cross beams for scaffolding, with plywood over that to keep from making a misstep. For joints, keep the compressed edges of the sheetrock together everywhere you can; it makes taping and bedding much easier. The hardest part is cutting out for fixtures.

For the taping and bedding, you can buy powdered mix and add water, or ready-to-use mud in five-gallon containers. The little extra cost is negligible compared to the convenience of not having to mix the stuff. Apply a light coat of mud over the seam and lay the tape into the mud. Press it into place with a 4" or so putty knife, making sure no air bubbles remain. Add another coat of mud and use a wider trowel to spread it. The trowel should span the compressed edges, leaving the mud level with the raised portion of the sheetrock. Where your joints are not compressed edges, feather the mud out with a wide trowel. I carefully pressed mud around the edges of the sheetrock where it meets the beams, then wiped the excess off the beams with a damp rag. Later, to trim out the ceilings I cut strips from walnut and used a router to give them a quarter-round appearance.

Allow a full day for the mud to set, lightly sand, and apply a second coat. The first-coat sanding does not have to be perfect so long as the imperfections are below the final surface. The second coat will fill in gaps. This coat must be sanded well, but be sure not to damage the sheetrock. For most people, two coats are sufficient, but a perfect job requires careful examination and touchup applications.

For the sanding, you may use a rough sponge and water. This does a good job and eliminates dust but is messy. Sandpaper is the usual other option, but someone discovered that screen wire is even better. Now you can buy pieces of screen cut to fit and a tool to hold it, including an extension handle that will keep you from having to climb up and down ladders. That done, you may paint or wallpaper.

If you prefer paneling, you do not have to tape and bed the sheetrock. To apply paneling without sheetrock requires heavy enough material to support itself. If you use thin paneling, it will sag unless you put up sheetrock first and bond the paneling to the sheetrock with adhesive.

Kitchen cabinets

Kitchen cabinets can be purchased at a building supply store. The unfinished ones are much cheaper than finished ones. They can be installed quickly and look professional. If you choose to go this route, spend some time at a supplier before you begin building to determine what sizes are available and adjust your design to accommodate them.

The other option is to build your own cabinets. This is not terribly difficult unless you want designs on your doors, which requires various passes with a router.

I ran into a bit of luck which caused me to decide to build my own. We had a nasty ice storm in Nashville, causing a friend to lose a large walnut tree. He gave me the wood in return for removing it from his property. I cut the timber

into 1-bys and stored it in a barn attic to cure, then used it to build my cabinets (photo 18). I had enough lumber to build all the framing, including sides, but not enough for the insets in the doors. For those, I purchased a sheet of unfinished ¼" oak plywood.

A how-to book, again, will give details about building cabinets. To sum up the process, for the upper cabinets 1 x 2 wood strips are nailed to the wall and ceiling and the cabinets are hung from these strips. For the lower cabinets, a level platform is constructed and attached to the floor and wall, then the cabinets are built on the platform.

Each cabinet door consists of a rectangular frame, routed on the inside edges to receive the insert (for me, oak plywood). The inserts are not glued but left free for expansion and contraction. Various designs can be added with a router as desired.

The countertop can be purchased ready to install, as in most new homes, or can be made from tile or other material. If you make the countertop, 3/4" plywood forms the base. For tile--and perhaps other materials--concrete sheets made for the purpose are screwed on top of the plywood. The concrete receives the adhesive material better than wood.

I found a good supply of ceramic tile in a garage sale for $10 and had enough both for the cabinet top and to put under my wood-burning stove and firewood holder. It is not glazed as cabinet tile should be, but sealers are made to solve the problem.

128

Flooring and other stuff

You have a multitude of flooring options: hardwood, vinyl that looks for all the world like hardwood, inlaid vinyl sheets, vinyl tile and ceramic tile of many qualities and designs, and carpet. This is a matter of taste.

Interior door assemblies are so inexpensive that the whole thing, including face boards, are cheaper than you can build them yourself. They also save a lot of time. If you choose to build your own, see the previous instructions.

I used wide walnut planks to close in the stair treads, which I then carpeted, leaving the oak risers showing. The treads also are of oak, and I had intended to leave them exposed, but in spite of curing for three years and my best efforts, the oak warped and shrunk. It had to be covered (photo 19, back cover) but looks quite good.

Window facings can be done any manner that pleases you. A good process is to start by attaching a face against the wall under the window and extending beyond the window on each side. A window sill is attached next; it is nailed to the window frame up against the closed sash and extending about an inch beyond the lower board. It should be wide enough, with cutouts on each side, to continue beyond the side facings for about an inch. The top face may be flush with the side faces or extend slightly beyond. Draw sketches to get a feel for what you want. I decided narrow facings would look better with timber and beam than regular 1 x 4 facings (photo 20). I made mine of cherry, given me by another unfortunate friend who lost a tree to the same ice storm that provided me

20

the walnut.

I also lucked out on another porch. My next-door neighbor sold me the pressure-treated lumber very cheap when he replaced his deck with an addition. I also closed in the pier-and-beam foundation (photo 21), partly for aesthetic reasons but mainly for better insulation.

I was about through with my house, lacking only a few trim jobs which I did as the spirit moved me.

If you have always dreamed of building your own place, let me encourage you to get to it. The experience is a wonderful one, even if, like me, you won't want to do it again.